I Have Never Seen

PARIS

But I Have Seen

BIGFOOT

A True Documentary of Bigfoot

Nancy Moosburner MS

Printed in the United States of America

First Printing September 2016

ISBN 978-1-945172-75-5 Paperback

ISBN 978-1-945173-38-7 eBook

Published by: Book Services
www.BookServices.us

Contents

⊞ = Photographs

Dedication

I dedicate this book to those persons who have had the courage to step forward and tell their true stories and experiences. Without other authors' books on the subject of Bigfoot, I would not have been able to understand the learning situation I was in. I believe each new book adds something to the big picture of the Bigfoot mystery. Staying open-minded is crucial to continued learning.

Nancy Moosburner

Introduction

It was my husband's dream to design and build our retirement home. This would be the second home we would design and build. For me, the first time was enough to last a lifetime.

I was happy living on a horse ranch in Nevada. We had fixed up a bunk house, so our son could have friends over, and the kids would have their own space. A four-stall barn housed our son's first horse, as well as our Angora rabbits, chickens, ducks, and watch-dog geese. I was an amateur beekeeper and had two hives on our three acres. We were surrounded by fields: a sheep ranch in front of our home and a dairy farm at the end of the private dirt road. We also had two dogs, two cats, and a hamster. I got involved with the 4-H Club with my son. My daughter and I took spinning lessons, which was why we had Angora rabbits. I made pies and applesauce from our apple trees and tended many gardens, including an herb garden. I worked for the local school district as an administrator, a job I loved. I was having fun being "Rebecca Home-Eca" on the ranch—until the day my husband came home with an announcement. He had an opportunity to retire early. As a result, he wanted to move to Washington State and build our retirement home.

I told my husband that would be fine with me, as long as if I didn't have to come along. I did not want to build a house again. Such a project preempts your time—all of it. I knew it would take the rest of our lives to finish everything. Moreover, all the money we earned would be funneled into this house project. Although we had purchased the property several years before this with the intent to build, the reality of actually *doing* it did not make me happy. I thought we should spend our money traveling and seeing the world. That would include Paris.

Our two older children had graduated from college, married, and were on their own. Our youngest son had one more year of high school, and he would be off to college. It was time for us to enjoy ourselves without children. I was so unhappy about building another house, I gave serious thought to going my separate way.

Upon further consideration, I believed that if my husband ended up with another woman while building this house, I would have to kill him. Then I would have to go to prison, so I did not have any choice except to buck up and build another house. So I went kick-

Introduction

ing and screaming all the way to the Pacific Northwest and ten acres of Olympic Rainforest.

The house took nine months to build. During construction, I discovered footprints in the dirt as the site was bulldozed and cleared for the house project. The footprints were clearly human-looking, but larger. Was it a Bigfoot? Perhaps. The possibility led me down a path of intense study and observation. I wanted to learn as much as I could about these wonderful animals.

Included in this book are most of the incidents that happened over a twenty-year period. Bigfoot is very, very real. Looking back, I feel honored to have seen this animal so many times, even though I have never seen Paris.

4

The highest form of ignorance is when you reject something you do not know anything about.

Wayne Dyer

Chapter 1
When Seconds Become Hours

My First Sighting of Bigfoot

I am standing nude in my second-floor bedroom, and I feel urine trickling down my leg. I am frozen in disbelief at what I am seeing out the window. The full moon is shining like a bright solar beam from the east. It is so bright that it is like daylight at 11:00 p.m. in the Pacific Northwest woods.

There was Bigfoot! He crawled from the woodsy slope in front of our house and slowly walked across the front yard to the back of our house and into the back woods.

This huge animal slowly strolled nonchalantly across the front lawn, apparently in no hurry, walking on two legs like a human. Its head was round as a basketball and sat on top of an eight- or nine-foot body. There was no apparent neck. The ears were like human ears, the lips were like human lips, the eyes were large and round; the nose was like a human nose, only larger, in keeping with the proportions of this animal. The arms were long and swaying slightly. The hands were like human hands; they were black with no fur on them. The rest of the body, including the face, was covered in black fur. I knew then that it was true: Bigfoot was alive and very well indeed.

I didn't know anything about Bigfoot. I had wondered if the stories of its existence were true or not. I joked with the electrician as he was wiring our new home. He asked if I wanted motion-detector lights in front of the garage and around the house. I told him that of course we wanted lights like that. If Bigfoot came around, I wanted to be able to see him. Washington State was well-known for its Bigfoot sightings, but was it really true?

I thought that knowing yes, Bigfoot is true, or no, Big Foot is not true, would be the end of the story. However, finding out that the stories were true was really only the beginning of my story. I did not know that at the time.

I was very busy with my life as an administrator for a school district, and I commuted to the Seattle area from southern Washington for work. Our ten acres were part of a parcel of close to a hundred acres of the Olympic Rainforest. There were only three houses within this hundred-acre parcel. If Bigfoot were alive and well, this would be his environment. There were plenty of munchy, crunchy things all around to eat.

There were elk, deer, raccoons, and opossums, and dozens of other mammals in the northwest woods, not to mention grouse and a myriad of other flying creatures.

Overview of the property

It took us ten years to complete all our house projects: decks, patios, gardens, landscaping, decorating, and furnishings. After twelve years of my working as a school administrator, we both retired to this secluded home and lived there for seven-and-a-half additional years, thus living a total of almost twenty years on this property. During the winters of our retirement years, we spent six months in southern Arizona. Eventually, we decided to sell our Washington home and move permanently to Arizona. I knew it was time for me to tell my Bigfoot stories.

My husband is a civil engineer and has a black-and-white way of looking at life. He believes that there is an explanation for everything, and anything that smacks of the paranormal is unreasonable. One of the reasons I married him was because I thought he was an open-minded and independent thinker. He always looks at both sides of an issue, wanting to understand the whole picture before making any decisions.

My Bigfoot sighting and the entire Bigfoot issue was too much for him to understand and accept. He thought I was losing my marbles. Of course, this made me angry. After all, I was his wife. Why would I bother with such a story if it were not true? I felt his attitude was disrespectful, considering the fact that in my job, I had handled one hundred employees and millions of dollars successfully! Well, if I *were* losing my marbles, it would cross over into other things in my life. Anyway, he could not handle this issue, and I remained angry at him for a very long time.

As a result, I was motivated to find proof that would pass his eagle-eyed scrutiny. How could I prove to my husband that Bigfoot was not only alive and well, but living on our property?

I rummaged around in my closet and found an old tape recorder from night school classes. Much to my surprise, the batteries still worked. The recorder was voice-activated, and I put it in my front bedroom window. I wanted to record any noise that Bigfoot made and prove to my husband that Bigfoot was real. In the end, I was glad that my husband would not believe me, because these recordings were the beginning of unraveling some Bigfoot mysteries. They give me reason to believe that I have something to share.

Chapter 2
Invisibility

Let's get right to the good stuff! Bigfoot can make himself invisible and he can stay that way if he chooses.

The information highway was just becoming a practical reality when I started studying Bigfoot. I discovered the Big Foot Researchers Organization (BFRO), founded by Matt Moneymaker. This is a site where people can share their Bigfoot experiences, anonymously if they choose, since many people feel they will be made fun of if they share their stories with friends and family. I am sure that I too will be made fun of, but I am seventy years old now and do not really care. (I would care, however, if I were still working.)

I started saving some of the reports that were sub-mitted to BFRO describing Bigfoot behavior and diet. Many observers reported driving down a dark road at night, or even in daylight, turning a bend in the road, and seeing Bigfoot crossing the road. I wanted more evidence than that. I found the stories of invisibility especially intriguing.

One article stated that a woman was hiking in the woods when she saw a Bigfoot standing on a rock. Next to it was a second Bigfoot with only one arm showing. The rest of its body was invisible. I thought that anyone who believed that was certifiably insane. Anyone could submit to this site, and I thought this was a joke submitted by someone with way too much time on their hands. That was how I felt—until it happened to me! I immediately dug out the "one-arm" article and read it again, reading it with very different eyes and a new understanding.

My first invisibility sighting was on a Sunday afternoon in January. It was about 1:00 p.m., and I was standing on the back deck of my home in southern Washington. From the deck there was a slope of about five feet that led into the woods. On the deck were two large pots, spaced four feet apart; there was a bench across the middle, the ends resting on the pots. (See picture on next page.) My golden retriever, Brutus, was making a funny barking sound with his head down. He was not a barky kind of dog, so his behavior got my attention. I stepped up on the bench, so I could see over the back slope into the woods. There was a Bigfoot walking down an old timber road toward our house! He was walking with his arms swaying and his head down, watching where he was going.

I froze as I watched this animal walk toward me. Even if I'd had a camera around my neck, I would not have been capable of snapping a picture. I couldn't move, and I could barely breathe. When the Bigfoot looked up and saw me, it turned to its right, where another timber road went uphill. It walked another ten feet and then stopped behind an alder tree about ten inches in diameter. I thought it was going to try to hide behind that skinny tree. Then, right before my eyes, it started to disappear. The process started from its left and right sides at the same time. Its body gradually became invisible from the outside toward the inside, until I could not see the Bigfoot any more. It was as if it wanted to make itself thin enough to hide behind that tree. Since there were no leaves on the trees at that time of year, I would have been able to see it bend over or kneel down if it tried to conceal itself on the ground. But that is not what happened. I was glad I had read that article about Bigfoot invisibility. Otherwise, I might have thought I was losing

Bench of boards laid across flowerpots

my mind. This was only the first time I experienced this phenomenon; there were others.

Another instance occurred after I had carried a dead chipmunk into the woods in front of our house. The poor chipmunk had drowned in the dog's water pail. I hated it when something like that happened, so I came up with a remedy. I established a twelve-month watering station appropriate for chipmunks and small critters.

In the case of the expired chipmunk, I was standing in our kitchen looking out the front of the house toward the Columbia River. We had three French doors in front of our kitchen table with two windows perpendicular to them. It was around 9:00 a.m. on a bright sunny day. A Bigfoot climbed up the slope from the woods in front of the house. It was holding the chipmunk in front of it with both hands. It slowly walked up the gravel path alongside our French vegetable garden and toward the driveway. It became visible through the first French door. As it walked toward the second French door, its whole body became lighter in color. When it reached the third door frame, its whole body looked like an old negative. By the time it had passed the door, it was almost invisible. As it appeared through the perpendicular windows next to the French doors, I saw that the Bigfoot had become completely invisible, and so had the chipmunk. This time, I saw the full body becoming invisible, not just a portion and then another portion.

I went outside later to investigate what I had seen. Because the Bigfoot was walking on a gravel pathway, I could see its footprints embedded in the gravel. I could follow the prints of a left foot and a right foot. I followed the footprints all the way to the driveway. So, although the Bigfoot became invisible halfway down the path, its weight still made impressions in the gravel for the entire distance. Its pace was casual, and I could easily step comfortably into each footprint.

On another occasion, Brutus was leaping like a deer among the waist-high ferns in the woods on the west side of the house, as if looking for something. I was in the office on the second floor. As I watched this leaping game from the office window, I saw a black hand wrap itself around a large fern, as if to look around, presumably for the dog. It almost looked like Brutus and the Bigfoot were playing a game of tag. The rest of the Bigfoot's body was invisible. I knew it was a Bigfoot hand I was looking at, as I had seen this hand before on my first Bigfoot sighting. I didn't know if this Bigfoot would hurt my dog, so I called Brutus. He left the woods and came obediently. Bigfoot seemed to have a mischievous and playful personality at times. However, this was an animal powerful enough to kill anything it wanted to. I had read some accounts of Bigfoot killing dogs, usually dogs that were bothering them, like dogs can.

By that time I was getting used to this invisibility effect of Bigfoot. The story could go on and on with all that I learned from my firsthand experiences. If you block this part out, you will learn nothing more about the reality of Bigfoot and its capabilities. Had I not had so many personal experiences, I might have been skeptical myself.

One day, my husband and I were picking fruit from an Italian plum tree growing along our driveway, which was almost a mile back from the highway. We had planted an orchard of several varieties of fruit trees along that part of our driveway. The plum tree produced a bumper crop of hundreds of pounds of plums almost every year.

As we were filling our baskets, I felt increasingly uncomfortable—like I was being watched. I thought I heard a disgruntled vocalization, but I could see nothing. Then, in a flash, something invisible ran swiftly between my husband and me, past the plum tree, and down the slope into the woods on the east. I could feel the wind on my face as this invisible creature ran by, passing about three feet from me. Although there was no noise, grasses along the edge of the slope were moving, due to the disturbance. Nothing else was moving. It was a beautiful, calm day. The dirt was somewhat scuffed up, but there were no footprints, as it had been dry, and the ground was hardened clay.

I was certain that this was a Bigfoot, and I sensed that it was afraid of us, as I was of it. Never to my knowledge did any Bigfoot ever take fruit from any of our fruit trees, including the wonderful apple trees in front of our house. Some have reported seeing Bigfoot eating apples, but they never bothered ours. I have also heard that apples are used as bait for expeditions searching for Big Foot.

On the other hand, we did have a large resident porcupine that would climb an apple tree, eat half an apple and throw it on the ground, then pick another apple and eat half of that one. There were plenty of fallen apples on the ground, but neither the deer nor any other wildlife ever ate them.

We also had a fifty-foot-long French vegetable garden in which I grew all kinds of vegetables. Never did we have a problem with any of the wildlife helping themselves to our produce. We never put food out for Bigfoot or for any of the wildlife, with the exception of the birds. We did feed many hummingbirds, and we put seeds out during the winter for the wild birds that stayed in the Northwest all winter. Putting food out for Bigfoot would have been creating a bond of trust with humans, which I did not think was a good idea. Feeding wildlife is not recommended, and in some places it is even illegal. It is well-known that bears can get into the habit of breaking into houses and cars for food. If bears could do that, so could Bigfoot. I did not want that problem. I had read a BFRO article about some hunters who had observed a Bigfoot chasing a bear out of his territory. If a black bear can force its way into someone's home, I can only imagine how easy it would be for a Bigfoot. An animal that powerful could also have harmed us.

The morning after the plum-tree incident, I opened the front door to begin my day with feeding the dog.

French vegetable garden

When I opened the door, I could feel a presence, but I couldn't see anything. However, I could smell something—the stench of a Bigfoot. I suspected it knew what time I opened the door every morning to take care of the dog. It seemed as if it were waiting for me. I closed the door and did not go outside for awhile. When I went outside later, the stench was gone, and so was the feeling of a presence.

One beautiful summer morning I was out on the back deck, and I could hear two men talking. I looked up and saw two heads about twenty feet from me passing through our property. Now I hate trespassers. I lived on ten acres in the middle of nowhere because I liked it like that. I put up No Trespassing signs all over the place. However, many hunters paid no attention to the signs, so there was always a problem. I yelled at the two men, telling them that they were trespassing on private property. They ducked down behind the bushes. My dog ran over to the shrubbery, barking, and then ran right back to me. I was not about to personally confront anyone, so I stayed where I was. That seemed like the end of the story. I assumed the two men left the property. When I examined the spot where I had seen the trespassers later, I realized that they would have to have been eight- or nine-feet tall for me to even see the tops of their heads. By yelling and startling them, I had missed what I believe to have been two Bigfoot talking and walking together.

Later in the afternoon of the same day, I was working in the rose garden near the back woods, when I heard the heavy footfalls of something walking around. I could hear sticks breaking and dead leaves crackling under their footsteps. I could see nothing. The area was open and clear for viewing. Any animal or person could have easily been seen. My best guess is that the two Bigfoot, and not two trespassing men, made themselves invisible to me and continued on their path into the woods, where they spent most of the day. Just because one does not always *see* Bigfoot, it does not mean that they are not there. One should remain open-minded.

About ten feet from the edge of my garage was a tree common to the Pacific Northwest, an enormous bigleaf maple with leaves twelve or more inches across and a canopy that was around 40 feet wide. The trunk of this tree was three-to-four feet in diameter. I always felt that a Bigfoot was in residence there, even though I could see nothing. As I walked by this tree each day, I would say, "I know you are there, Bigfoot. I can smell you!" The powerful musty odor was unmistakable.

One day I was calling my cat, Sally, to come in for her nap. I wanted her to be near me at all times, so I could keep an eye on her. However, she would wander off from time to time. I was very worried about her, and I continued calling her name for almost half an hour. This would be sleeping time for Bigfoot, according to the researchers, most of whom have concluded that Bigfoot is a nocturnal animal. I finally heard a loud sigh from behind the bigleaf maple tree, the kind of sigh that sounds like "shut up and stop bothering me." I knew I was right about that Bigfoot. On another occasion, I heard a whining sound from a youngster and a *shhhh* sound from what may have been a female Bigfoot. I was working in the garden in front of this maple tree, and my husband was using the loud and scary weed trimmer at the time. I think that may have provoked the Bigfoot's whining. (Sally did finally return to the house.)

There was other, more positive proof of the big animal's unseen presence. I walked out on my brick patio early one morning. To get to the brick patio, I had to walk over a wooden deck which was covered with morning dew. I reached the patio and continued around to the west side of our house, walking on a manor-stone garden wall. Suddenly there was a rush of branches and twigs breaking. Something had run from the front brick patio into the west part of the woods and then walked around the back of the house through the woods directly over to the bigleaf maple.

Bigleaf maple tree

When I went back to the brick patio, I could see wet barefoot prints on the brick. Bare feet had walked over the dew-covered wooden deck and onto the brick, leaving the footprints. I believe it was the Bigfoot that was hanging out at the maple tree by the garage. The footprints were long and thin, more like those of a female Bigfoot, rather than the bigger and wider footprints of a male. If this Bigfoot had stayed her course, we would have bumped right into each other, probably scaring the living daylights out of both of us. She would not have seen me, since I was around the corner of the house on the garden wall.

When I walked this way I often heard wood-knocking from different parts of the woods. I wondered if some of the Bigfoot had seen me and were transmitting that message to their companions in other areas. On this occasion, I did not hear any wood-knocking, but

I am sure Bigfoot used a method of communication that was beyond the range of human hearing. However, the tape recorder picked up this communication, as I will discuss later.

Wooden deck transitioning to brick patio

One night, I put my tape recorder in the maple tree to see if I could record something during the night. I was hoping for a movement—anything. I got absolutely nothing. It was as if it was known that I had put the recorder there. I didn't even get a chipmunk scurrying around, a plane flying overhead, a dog barking, or a ship tooting its horn on the river. Although this Bigfoot was invisible to me, I knew she was there, day after day. She chose this site and stayed there for about two years, the last two years we lived in the house. She could still be there for all I know. It may seem strange that a Bigfoot would hang out right next to my house, making the area around the ancient maple her permanent home, but she was not the only one I shared my property with.

Bigfoot is well-known for knocking on wood as a means of communication. One afternoon, I was planting flowers under the bigleaf maple. I heard a loud motorcycle come down from our neighbor's driveway at the top of the hill and stop at the gate across our driveway which was closed and locked. This disturbing noise, especially on a quiet afternoon, which is generally naptime for Bigfoot, created some wood-knocking. About sixty feet from where I was working in the garden, I could hear wood-knocking on another bigleaf maple tree. The knocking sound came from around fifteen feet up the trunk. I could see absolutely nothing, not a woodpecker, not even a stick or a piece of wood that would make the knocking sound. I had a clear view directly to this tree. This could have been a male Bigfoot, and his female was probably the one that hung out at the maple tree next to the garage where I was working. Perhaps he was the lookout for his family, protecting them by staying close, though not in exactly the same place.

Because I had moved to Washington State from Nevada, I was enthralled with all the trees and greenery and the abundance of berries and nuts. Nevada's flora was primarily sagebrush, with the occasional cottonwood tree in town or ponderosa pine at higher elevations. I loved walking up the almost mile-long private drive in Washington with my dog. The drive was cut through the woods. I left a picnic bench at the pump house, about five-hundred feet from our home, so I would have a place to sit and ponder the beauty of my new surroundings.

Next to the picnic bench was a log along one side of the woods, right next to the driveway. I heard noises that sounded like a grouse coming from the log. I could not see a grouse or anything else that might make the noise. Every time I made a visit to the picnic bench, the grouse sound became louder and louder until the sound was as loud as a noisy motorcycle. It would make the hair stand up on my neck and arms. That was when I became aware that the sound was not being made by a grouse. Additional research into sounds made by Bigfoot turned up others who had heard this same sound, a sound something like a grouse. If a Bigfoot was there, I could not see it. It sounded as if the noise was right next to me as I sat on the bench. Now I think it was a Bigfoot, and that this was his claimed space. I will write more about claimed spaces later.

When I walked up the driveway with Brutus, he would very often bark at something and then go on a chase. I could see nothing that the dog was barking at or chasing. I tried walking in a squatting position, so I would be at the same height as the dog's eyes. I still couldn't see anything of interest. I have pondered whether our dog had the ability to see Bigfoot even though I could not. I remember an episode of the television program *Unsolved Mysteries* in which a man put three colors of lenses on his camera. He was able to take pictures of round protoplasmic-like things flying through the air. These protoplasmic objects were not visible to the human eye. I wonder if a similar technique would reveal an invisible Bigfoot? Such an experiment might yield interesting results on some of the Bigfoot expeditions. So much to learn and so much to try!

My goodbye to Bigfoot came as a surprise just before I left Washington to take up permanent residence in Arizona. It was the afternoon before we were to leave our home of almost twenty years and take off for a new life in Arizona. I was home alone. I walked to my back deck and, hanging onto the railing, I yelled into the wind, "Goodbye, Bigfoot! I'm moving to Arizona. There are new people moving into our house. They have a dog, so be nice to it. They do not know you are here, and maybe they never will. I did not tell them about you. Good-bye. I love you!"

I sighed, "Oh well," as I walked to the side of the garage to go back into the house. And then I got an answer back! This was Bigfoot, not visible, but actually talking to me. It was not in English or samurai chatter, as recorded by other researchers. It was in very guttural sounds. Some of the vocalizations sounded like Bigfoot opened its mouth very wide and made sounds from its throat without the use of a tongue. I had never heard these sounds in any of my recordings. They were loud and intentional. Since I understood nothing, I clapped my hands three times as they did in wood-knocking. Bigfoot always knocked three times.

This conversation went on for about two minutes. Three times I clapped my hands in response. I then walked into the house and upstairs. It all seemed so natural—a conversation with Bigfoot. Then it hit me! Oh my God! Bigfoot had talked back to me! This communication had not happened to me before. Normally, I would have had my second recorder in the back window of the bedroom recording this conversation, but it was already packed away for the move to Arizona. Sadly, I did not get a recording of this response. Again, Bigfoot was completely invisible.

The sound seemed to be only about five feet from me. Bigfoot was at the top of the five-foot slope, and I was at the bottom. It obviously knew something was going on. As part of our landscaping, we had eight outside rooms with tables and chairs in each of them. So many things were being moved around; there was an unusual level of outside activity. So it seems I had lived in a zoo, being watched by Bigfoot. It accepted our co-habitation arrangements, whether it liked it or not, and it never harmed me or my animals. I always showed respect. I never wanted anything, except to try to understand their way of life, just as they were interested in my way of life.

Chapter 3
The Raven and Gifting

Fifty feet up in a Douglas fir tree that looks into the entrance of our home, sat a raven. It was crowing non-stop at our dog, Brutus. I thought maybe the raven had tried to get at the corn in the vegetable garden, and the dog was trying to chase it away. Brutus was barking furiously and, out of keeping with his temperament, he was even growling at the bird. He started running down the front slope after the raven. I could hardly understand what was going on. Since Brutus was not a vicious, aggressive or barking kind of dog, his behavior surprised me. As I was trying to figure out what was happening, I looked up at the raven and got a chilling and hateful message from the bird. It was as if it were communicating with me telepathically. "I hate you. I'm going to get you. I am going to kill you. Get out of here!" I was taken aback. *What had just happened?* I felt threatened and profoundly uncomfortable, and I think Brutus felt the same way.

Chapter 3 - The Raven and Gifting

The following Friday, I came home from work, and there was the raven on the doorstep of the entrance to our house. The raven was dead. There was not a wing broken. There was not a feather out of place, nor any blood or sign of a struggle, no broken neck. It looked like a healthy bird, only it lay dead on my doorstep.

Subsequent to that incident, I have found articles explaining that a Bigfoot can physically be in one place, but at the same time transform its spirit into another place or animal, such as a bird. The bird acts as a drone for Bigfoot, inspecting the landscape for intruders into its territory and probably also scouting the area for food, such as deer or elk.

Have you been hiking through the woods and suddenly become aware that you were being watched by a large bird, such as a raven, a hawk or an eagle? If you have, then you might understand my feeling that I was getting a specific message. It might make sense to you that the message I received from the Raven—I hate you, I am going to kill you—was actually a message from Bigfoot. Essentially, we had moved into what I call a Bigfoot compound. Our acreage was already an established housing area for many Bigfoot. They did not like my co-habiting with them when we first moved in. I could certainly understand where they were coming from. I moved into their territory, removed many trees, and displaced their established spaces.

Bigfoot would pound on our house repeatedly. One time a Bigfoot pounded on our house so hard that the vibrations knocked open some plastic drawers that were against the inside garage wall. One of the plastic drawer units fell on the floor, spilling its contents. I knew it was a Bigfoot because its stench lingered under the roof of our front porch, which is next to the garage. Its pounding on the house was definitely a message. *Get out of here! you are in my territory!*

In Lisa A. Shiel's book, *Backyard Bigfoot*, she describes the gifting behavior of Bigfoot. After reading her book, I started connecting the dots and realized that the dead raven left on my doorstep was probably a gift from Bigfoot. After receiving such a hateful message, the gifting was deeply perplexing.

The Friday following the raven incident, I found a dead rabbit waiting for me on my door step. The rabbit had been slit down the front with great precision. All the entrails had been removed. The skin had been pecked completely clean, as if to leave a skin of value. The head, the tail, and the legs were intact. At the time, I had absolutely no idea where this rabbit skin could have come from or why it had been delivered to my door step. However, I now understand that it was probably another gift from Bigfoot.

Bigfoot seemed to be everywhere on our property, watching me all the time. One of our landscaping chores was raking up all the pinecones and pine needles, as well as the leaves. One midsummer morning I stepped out of the house to find a pile of pinecones in the driveway. Pinecone-raking season was long gone. It was not something that needed to be done in the middle of summer. However, there was no disputing the presence of a substantial pile of pinecones. I believe this was a gift from Bigfoot. Ron Morehead, in his book, *Voices in the Wilderness,* relates that he also was gifted with a pile of pinecones during his camping experience with Bigfoot.

Around the corner of our driveway was a row of rhododendrons that I pruned every year. As I worked, I would leave the trimmings along the driveway to rake up later, at the end of the project. My husband always assisted me with the cleanup, a project that took the better part of a day.

The day after we cleaned up my trimmings, I was walking up the driveway to admire the my newly-pruned rhododendrons. Lo and behold, there was a pile of twigs and related debris on the opposite side of the driveway from where I had been working. I knew this had not been left by either my husband or me, as we had driven past the shrubs early in the evening before, on our way into town for dinner. We would have noticed the pile of debris at that time. I believe this was another gift from Bigfoot, and that he was copying my behavior.

Chapter 4
Recordings and Bigfoot Spacings

Over the years, I became increasingly familiar with the habits of Bigfoot, both from my personal experiences and from recording them for years from locations in the front of our home, the back of our home, and in our woods. I read everything that was available. I learned some very interesting things. One of the most important things I learned from my personal observations and my daily recordings was that a Bigfoot stays very close to home twenty-four hours a day, seven days a week, year in and year out. It is territorial and not a wanderer. I believe this is new information, as I have not read or heard of this from any other researcher or author.

Each Bigfoot owns a personal tree and a surrounding space that they have chosen for themselves. They keep this tree and the surrounding area of about fifty feet as theirs forever. They do not move around to different areas to live. The same Bigfoot animals were at the same trees and spaces for the almost twenty years I lived in my southern Washington home.

I was able to name the different Bigfoot because of their personality characteristics, which I picked up on the tape recordings. Some of the sounds could be heard by humans, but most could not. Sometimes a Bigfoot would take off for a couple days from their permanent place, but they always returned to their tree space and the area that they had claimed for themselves.

I researched gorillas and found that they too have their own areas that are spaced about fifty feet from other gorillas, just like Bigfoot. It makes sense that Bigfoot does not need to move from their area for food. Resources for food remain available twelve months of the year in the Pacific Northwest. There are always elk and deer in the woods, fish in the river, and green things available year round. I wonder if this behavior is specific to the area where my house was located. Maybe in other geographic areas, Bigfoot would need to move around because their food resources are not constant from season to season. I believe Bigfoot is a social animal and may visit their relatives or friends in other areas, just as we do. Each Bigfoot is unique, just as people are.

Drummer

The Bigfoot who lived directly in front of our home I called Drummer. Every time it rained, Drummer would make a drum sound like a water drip, but louder than a rain drop. At first I thought there was a leak in the roof, but as I listened carefully the sounds were too rhythmical and timed precisely. To my delight, one very calm summer evening when there was no rain, Drummer started drumming. It sounded like he was using a deer skull and a stick. Well, he drummed out a musical and rhythmical sound that lasted for a couple minutes. And I got it on my tape recorder! That was the first time I heard a recital like that. At that point, I knew I was right about Drummer.

At other times, he would do some drumming in response to something happening in the environment. For example, if a plane were flying over the property, he would respond with his drumming sound, as well as mimicking the sound of the plane with his mouth. Drummer lived down the slope directly in front of our house, probably fifteen feet from the edge of the cliff. I had two daylight sightings of a large dark cinnamon brown Bigfoot from the front of the house, and it may have been Drummer. He may have been the same Bigfoot that I had seen becoming invisible while carrying the dead chipmunk. The chipmunk-carrying Bigfoot had been the same cinnamon brown color until, of course, it became invisible. It had the same round basketball head with no apparent neck, human-like ears, long arms, and hands without fur.

Another time I was moving the hose and sprinkler around on the front lawn. I was very close to the edge of the front slope, which leads into the woods and Drummer's area. I was near a large hemlock tree that stood at the edge of the lawn where it meets the woods. I placed the hose close to the tree, walked about thirty

34

feet from the tree to the front deck, and turned around to pull up the water pump handle to start the sprinkler. When I turned around, facing the hemlock tree, there was a cinnamon-brown Bigfoot sitting under the tree. As I was placing the sprinkler on the front lawn, I was probably eight feet away from this Bigfoot. My heart felt like it just stopped when I saw Bigfoot watching me. If he had not made a movement, I do not think I would have noticed him. Bigfoot can blend in with their environment extremely well. He moved his left shoulder to turn around and go back down the slope in front of our house. He could easily have done me in, but he did nothing. He had just been watching me, not stalking me. Drummer was the only Bigfoot I recorded making a drumming sound.

Clicker

The Bigfoot that lived in the southwest corner of our property, I named *Clicker*. We had a patio under a large bigleaf maple tree in front of her space behind our house. Whenever we got too close, she would click rapidly with her tongue. I recorded this often. Sometimes I would leave my tape recorder on the edge of this back patio all day long. In the evening, I would go to retrieve my tape recorder. When I got close to the edge of the woods, Clicker would start clicking. I could hear my own footsteps on the tape recorder as I retreated to my house, and I could hear Clicker clicking as I walked.

I also had a rose garden in an area next to a patio. One Sunday I was working all day in the garden. I was on my knees most of the time, and I could see into the woods because I was at such a low level. As I knelt in the garden, I could hear Clicker walking toward me, breaking small twigs as she walked. I looked into the woods at the outside edge of the rose garden, which was about three feet from me, and I could see Clicker walking in a squatting position to a place where she could watch me better. She was a greyish-brown color, somewhat small in stature. Her small stature was what made me think she was a female. I recorded her year after year in this same area. She was in the area for the entire twenty years that we lived on this property. I never recorded another Bigfoot that made the same clicking sounds.

One day Clicker threw a stone for my entertainment, while I was working in the rose garden. I had been digging up clay all day. I would dump the clay into a plastic pail and dump it into the wheelbarrow. My husband then wheeled the clay away to dispose of it. I was anxious to replace the clay in the garden with good topsoil, so the roses would grow better. Because I only had the weekend to work on this project, I was out there all day long trying to finish it. Now, I considered this to be very brave of me, because I knew a Bigfoot was there. I knew about Clicker, but I did not know the level of her tolerance for me. Finally, as I was sitting on the stone wall in front of the rose garden for a break, Clicker threw a one-inch round stone furiously to the ground and made a get-out-of-here noise. Out of respect, I retreated until the next day.

Rose garden with ladybug house

At the back edge of this rose garden, there was an alder tree about five inches in diameter. My husband sawed the tree down, leaving the roots in the ground and a four-foot piece of the tree intact. I purchased a very nice ladybug house, which we put on top of the thin alder stump. We installed the ladybug house just before dinner one evening. About an hour later, after dinner, I was strolling among our gardens and went to admire the ladybug house. I found it smacked in half and part of it lying on the ground. Well, guess who did that? I decided I was pushing my luck with Clicker by staying much too long and too close to her space and permanent territory. At least Clicker did not smack *me* in half!

At one point, my husband installed a surveillance system for me. The surveillance system sent recordings to a video player set up inside the house. One

Sunday afternoon I was reviewing the videotape from the weekly surveillance, and I saw Clicker walking on the sidewalk which curled around the house. Well now I knew she was a female, and I knew she was Clicker by her coloring. The problem was that I had switched the recorder into view mode which meant the recording mode was off. So I have no permanent record of her!

The main problem with this surveillance system was the delay. There was a thirty-second delay and nothing of consequence was ever recorded.

Whiney

Whiney lived about 500 feet up our driveway away from the house. I always heard him whining while I was lying in the hammock at the edge of our culinary herb garden.

One day I was pruning a holly tree next to his space. I had planted a row of six holly trees along the driveway, and only five of them had been pruned the previous year. The five holly trees that had been pruned were now taller and bigger than the one that had not. So getting up there and pruning that last holly had been on my "to do" list for a long time. As I started pruning, I could hear a low and long whine. I knew it was Whiney. Judging from the sound, he was about 25 feet from me. I could see nothing.

Since Bigfoot had never hurt me or my animals, I decided to continue pruning the tree. Soon I heard another longer and louder whine, although it was still soft for a Bigfoot. I just kept on pruning. Then another louder and longer whine came my way. I had almost finished pruning the holly and was determined to continue until I was done. This time there was an extremely loud and long whine that made the hair stand up on my neck and arms. I swung the long-handled pruners over my shoulder and quickly walked down the driveway to the house. Later that afternoon, at about 4:00 p.m, I walked back up the driveway to the hollies. The tree I was pruning had been snapped in half. I think it is probably better to listen to Bigfoot the first time and leave the area immediately when co-habiting with him. Big Foot rules! This was just like Clicker smacking my ladybug house. If I had left sooner, the ladybug house may not have been broken. If I had shown more respect for Whiney and left immediately, the holly tree would not have been snapped in half.

There was one time when poor Whiney had reason to whine. The property adjacent to ours was being cleared for a building site for two homes. The eastern adjacent property line was about 300 feet from our driveway and part of it was in Whiney's permanent space. Men were using chain saws all day long, logging the five-acre property. It was about 6:00 p.m. on that summer day. I was lying in the hammock next to the herb garden closest to Whiney's' space. He had returned to his space after the day-long racket from the chain saws. Whiney let out a loud whine that would break your heart. He was absolutely devastated to find his space mostly cleared of all the trees. It sounded as if he were actually crying with disbelief and horror at

39

what someone had done to his space. If I had walked around the corner of the driveway, I probably could have seen Whiney. I did not want him to think I was responsible for this logging. He could easily have killed me, especially under duress. I went into the house. I felt so sorry for Whiney. I wished I could purchase all the land and make it into a wildlife refuge.

Six months before we moved to Arizona, Whiney showed himself to me. He was in a sitting position in his space right along the driveway next to a bigleaf maple tree. My husband and I were driving up the driveway, when I noticed something dark next to the tree—something that I was not accustomed to seeing. When you live in these woods and walk through the property hundreds of times, you become familiar with every tree and bush and rock, especially if you are somewhat of a naturalist.

When we neared the dark spot, I saw the Bigfoot. Whiney was sitting with his head down, shaking it slightly, and looking at the ground. I think he was nervous about letting me see him, but for some reason, he had decided to do so. He looked up at me. He looked different from the basketball-head Bigfoot I had seen previously. His head was more like a normal human head. His big brown eyes were not round, but slightly slanted at the ends. They reminded me of my son's eyes. His hair was multi-colored, not black and not brown, and his face was covered with fur. The covering on the rest of his body was all the same length and color. I felt like he was saying hello. We continued driving past, not stopping. I wish we had stopped. However, seeing Bigfoot is always a surprise and it takes a little bit to comprehend what it was you just saw. You do not immediately say, "Oh look! There is Whiney!" The way it happens is you see Bigfoot, and you drive by; there is a process of thinking, in which you start to comprehend. And then it hits you: *I just saw Whiney!* Now I knew I had two different species of Bigfoot on my property. In my reading, I had come across different descriptions of Bigfoot. I'd read and think, "Nope. That isn't my Bigfoot. Now I know different.

Big Red

Big Red was a very tall and slender Bigfoot whose space was in the pump house area, about 500 feet from the house and 50 feet from Whiney's space. I first saw Big Red about two years after we moved into our home. I was walking up the driveway through the woods with my dog, very early in the morning. I was just going for a short walk before I had to leave for a meeting in Portland. The driveway was slightly uphill with a five-percent slope. The dog ran ahead of me up to the pump house and pond area. He started barking furiously, as if at something threatening. As I walked up the slope, I saw a red-colored Bigfoot. When he spotted me, he ran off into the woods through some water. When I checked the water, I could see a disturbance in the bottom of the pond area he had run through, but no footprints. I did not get a really good look at him at the time, because my sighting was so brief. However, I saw him a couple of more times over the years, and one of those times, I got a really good look at Big Red.

41

I Have Never Seen Paris but I Have Seen Bigfoot

One afternoon, my husband and I were coming home from town. The steep part of our driveway looks down into a deep ravine, where a herd of elk can often be seen resting. As we proceeded down the road, I saw Big Red to our right. He had heard our truck, so he camouflaged himself to look like a tree that had split in two. The way he was leaning on the tree, combined with the red of his fur, made him look like the inside of a reddish-colored tree with a limb split off. I said, "There's Big Red!" Although my husband was looking right at it, he believed it was a split tree. At the time, he was so in denial of the reality of Bigfoot! It was interesting how that "split tree" was not there later in the day. I asked my husband where that split tree went. He was completely silent.

Another time we were returning from town and about 50 feet from the house, when I saw Big Red standing on a slight slope on the right side of the driveway next to the rhododendrons. I know he could hear the truck coming down the driveway, but he didn't hide. It was as if he were again willing to let me see him.

I was sitting in the front passenger seat of the truck. Right next to my side, only about three feet away was Big Red standing in full view. He didn't have a basketball-shaped head and he did not have a head like Whiney. He was different. His hands had gray skin with no fur. His feet had gray skin with no fur. He did have a neck, and the shape of his face was very human-like. He was very tall—about ten feet tall—and slender. He did not have the muscular build of the other Bigfoot I had seen. I had seen drawings of

Bigfoot on the BFRO site and Big Red looked exactly like one of those pictures.

With this sighting, I realized I had three species of Bigfoot on my property: First, the ones with the basketball-shaped heads, then the ones that looked like Whiney, and now Big Red. Big Red and I stared briefly at one another. He then turned to his left to start up the slope, putting his hand parallel to the ground, pushing it down quickly, as if to say, "I don't have to worry about them." When he did this, I could see the long nails on his left hand. In less than a minute we were home. I jumped out of the truck and ran up the stairs of the back slope to look into the back woods, hoping to see more of Big Red. I could see nothing. He could not have walked out of my sight as I could see a great distance into the woods. My best guess is that he made himself invisible.

Stinky

Stinky was the Bigfoot that stayed by the bigleaf maple tree next to our garage. I called her name every day as I passed by the tree. The odor was like garbage that has had a chance to decompose for a couple of days. The scent was similar to the odor you sometimes smell at a zoo. I didn't talk to this Bigfoot except to say, "I know you are there, Stinky. I can smell you."

Clapper

Our small vineyard rested on the edge of a cliff overlooking the Columbia River. It was next to the herb garden along the driveway and about 80 feet from the house. On the opposite side of the road, across from the vineyard, was a row of rhododendrons. Behind them was the woods and deep brush. One day when I was pruning the grapes, leaving the vines along the driveway, I heard Clapper. There was definitely a Bigfoot in the brush right across the driveway from me. He had two stones and was clapping them together. I just froze. I knew it was a Bigfoot, and I had read that one of the things they do is clap stones together. I felt very far from the house, which was my safety net. Obviously Clapper had been sitting there watching me. I could see nothing. This Bigfoot was either in the brush, where I could not see him, or he was invisible. I just left and went home.

We always left our bedroom windows open at night, year round. Several times, I heard Clapper walking through the woods on the west side of our house. As he was walking, he was clapping stones together. I could hear the clapping grow louder as he drew close to the house and become fainter as he walked farther and farther into the woods. His space was across from the vineyard. He was the only Bigfoot I noticed that clapped stones together.

Chapter 5
Visitors from Other Places and Spaces

The Elephant

I was working in the rose garden behind the house in Clicker's territory, when I heard something that sounded like an elephant walking through the woods. I'd never heard a Bigfoot that sounded so heavy and ponderous. They did not make sounds like an elephant. However, there was no doubt that a large animal was slowly walking through the woods, breaking sticks and disturbing the thick foliage. I was not about to go into the woods to see what was there. I continued to work in my garden. With my work schedule, my time was limited, and I wanted to plant some roses that afternoon.

While I was working, Brutus trotted off into the woods in the direction of the sound. I didn't call him to come, because I sometimes second-guess myself, and then I feel silly. After all, I didn't know if something were there, or if it would still be there. The noise was coming from about one hundred feet from where I was working. After a few minutes, Brutus started barking wildly. It sounded like he'd seen something that had frightened, or perhaps, surprised him. Just as Brutus started barking, I heard a short scream, as if from a child—or a juvenile Bigfoot. I felt sure I was right about the Bigfoot presence. If there was a juvenile involved, I was afraid Bigfoot would kill my dog to protect her baby. I immediately called Brutus, and he obediently came running back to me. Brutus stayed with me while I finished my planting.

The following July I was home on vacation. I was alone, sitting at our kitchen table. My bare feet were dangling to the wood floor, barely touching the wood. Around the corner of the driveway, I heard those elephant footsteps again. They were advancing down the driveway toward the house from Whiney's space. I could feel the vibration from whatever was approaching with my bare feet where they touched the wood floor.

Sometimes, when an extra-large cargo ship went by on the Columbia River in front of our house, we could feel some vibrations from it. However, there were no cargo ships or any boat on the river at that time, and there were no planes going over the house. My view from the kitchen table was directly toward the river for a clear view of any river traffic. Although planes frequently passed back and forth on the river, they never caused any vibrations in our home. So what was it?

I considered driving down the incline to see what I could see. Then I thought, "No...I don't think so. *This animal sounds big enough to step on my car like it was an ant.*" I could only picture something the size of the supposedly extinct *Gigantopithecus,* an ape-like animal that was close to ten-feet tall and weighed as much as a Hereford bull. Only a Bigfoot that large—or an elephant—would cause my kitchen floor to vibrate so much. I looked for footprints later, but found nothing in the hard clay and large gravel of the driveway. I think this animal went straight to the edge of the cliff, instead of toward my house. I wasn't sure if this were a resident Bigfoot or a visitor.

Every Fourth of July weekend, a visiting Bigfoot would come around. Although I never saw this animal, I believe he was huge, like a *Gigantopithecus,* or even an elephant. He smelled like a skunk. The odor was so strong that I had to close every window in the house. I knew from experience that the stench would linger indefinitely in the house once it got in. To describe it as the smell of a skunk would be an understatement. It smelled more like one thousand skunks. It was hard to breathe; if you took a deep breath, you gagged. Sometimes I'd smell him behind the house and then he would move to the front of the house. He was not a resident of this property or I would have noticed him previously, simply from the smell.

It was scary. He could probably look into my second-story bedroom window when he was standing on the ground. He seemed like a real King Kong. I never saw him, but his stench said, "Get out of my way!" To the best of my knowledge, he only stayed one or two nights. He could have been the Bigfoot that had walked down the driveway and made vibrations on the kitchen floor.

Since he seemed to have gone towards the cliff, he could be a resident farther down the cliff-side. There was a sheer two-hundred-foot cliff in front of our house. He could also be the Bigfoot I had heard making elephant footsteps back by the rose garden. Therefore, he could have been a resident, but I did not know where his space was. It would have to be farther away, as his stench would have been very noticeable had he been closer.

Chapter 6
Additional Bigfoot Sightings

Double the Fun Sighting

Bigfoot can be invisible, but they can also be very visible. I made a list of my visible sightings. I had twenty-two sightings in about twenty years. This was not a bad record, since I only lived in this house on weekends and holidays until I retired. And then, I lived there only six months before moving to Arizona. I had one sighting that was not on our property.

It was June 1995 when I had my most impressive sighting of Bigfoot. Because I commuted to the Seattle area for work, I was always rushing to get gardening jobs done on the weekends. Now it was summer, and I was looking forward to spending my entire vacation gardening at a more leisurely pace. Don't call me, don't talk to me, don't ask me for anything, I'm gardening, just leave me alone.

I Have Never Seen Paris but I Have Seen Bigfoot

Before I could plant my flowers, I had to get rid of some weeds. I was with Brutus, spraying weeds on the west side of our house, towards the back. I could smell something very close to me. I thought it could be a Bigfoot. I was also convinced that if I told anyone that I thought there was a Bigfoot there, they would think I was losing it. The smell was only about five feet from me.

Brutus started sniffing around and headed for the wooded area. I told Brutus to stay with me and he did, at least for a while. However, I was spraying next to some fruit trees, watching the spray very closely, as I didn't want to get any spray on the trees. I was so intensely focused on my task that I lost track of Brutus. He had gone into the woods, and I could hear scrambling noises in the brush. Brutus was sniffing the ground along the manor-stone wall that separated the woods from my garden. Then I heard Brutus actually yell—not bark, but yell!

When I looked up, I saw the back of a black animal moving along the manor-stone wall. I thought it was a bear, and that I had better get out of there. I did not know of any safe and pleasant bear encounters. However, I forced myself to stay. If it were a Bigfoot, I wanted to see it.

After traveling about fifteen feet along the manor-stone wall, this dark furry animal stood up. Oh — my—gosh! It *was* a Bigfoot! "I'm dead," I thought. It was so huge, I felt as insignificant as an ant. I was choked with fear, but also paralyzed by my own curiosity; I actually had an out-of-body experience. I saw a double of myself, clothes and all, jump out of my body and stand next to me, also watching Bigfoot.

The Bigfoot stared straight ahead at the woods in front of the house, as if looking for me, and I could tell he was very keen. I could tell he knew what was going on all the time. Then he turned a little and stared at the front patio which swings around in the front of the house looking for me. He stared at the garden wall around the side and back of the house, still searching. When he did not see me, he turned his head to the left and looked directly at me.

Patio curving around house

I stood there like a frozen tree stump. We stared at each other for a few seconds. I do not think I was breathing. His yellow eyes were large and round. He had the basketball-shaped head and no neck. His other features—ears, nose, and lips—were very humanoid. The fur on his body was black, but there was no fur on his hands. This animal looked just like the Bigfoot I had seen in the moonlight from my bedroom window. The Bigfoot opened his mouth and made an oh! oh! facial expression, as if I had startled him! He turned his left shoulder towards me and held his left arm straight out. I could see the black hair hanging down, and I could see gray skin underneath the hair. He turned and ran into the woods with my dog right after him. I called to Brutus, but he didn't come when I called him this time. I was absolutely terrified! I heaved a sigh of relief when Brutus later came back unharmed.

I explored the spot where Bigfoot had been standing and was surprised to find that the height of this animal was greater than I had imagined. He was standing on a slight downward slope, where there was a tree limb he had to duck under. From the ground to this tree limb was ten feet. There were no footprints, as the ground was hard and covered with leaves.

I carefully looked over the manor-stone wall and saw where Bigfoot had been lying on the ground directly in front of me. During the construction of our new home, a bulldozer had made a wave with the dirt, leaving an alcove to curl up in if you were so inclined. I think Bigfoot had been taking his afternoon nap when Brutus and I disturbed him.

At that time, I did not yet know that Bigfoot actually lived in my backyard all the time. I just thought he was passing through, like a bear in the woods. I had a lot to learn at this point. Because I thought Bigfoot would be on his way, I continued spraying the weeds.

As for my out-of-body experience, as soon as Bigfoot turned and headed for the woods, the duplicate of me, my doppelganger, jumped back into my body. My clone was completely separate from me. I was looking at my clone and the clone was looking at Bigfoot. Was that my soul or my ghost? In any case, it was a "double the fun" experience for me.

You-Tarzan, Me-Jane Sighting

On Friday nights, when I came home from work for the weekend, one of the first things I did was to go upstairs and change the tapes in the two tape recorders I always left in my bedroom windows while I was gone. I would leave one recorder in the front of the house and one in the back window of the sleeping porch off the master bedroom.

One Friday, when I reached the window, I could see a Bigfoot at the edge of the woods standing next to our compost pile. We had just gotten home, so we were probably making a lot of noise and the Bigfoot was checking it out. I sat down next to the open window and started to talk to the Bigfoot. It was about 9:30 p.m., but I could clearly see its eyes because they were glowing red in the dark. And even though it was dark, I could see it quite well, standing up on the slope of our compost pile and looking at me. Since he stayed put, I started to talk to this animal.

"Hi Bigfoot. My name is Nancy. Can you say Nancy? What's your name? Can you talk to me? Can we be friends? I know you're there. I won't hurt you. Bigfoot just stood there staring at me. I would say he was a little sheepish and a little curious at the same time. After talking for about thirty minutes, I looked away for a second. When I looked back, the Bigfoot was gone. If he had wanted to communicate with me, he could have. He could have used mental telepathy or any kind of chatter or non-verbal communication. Kewaunee Lapseritis, in his book, *The Sasquatch People*, talks about having telepathic communications with Bigfoot. This could have easily happened to me, but it did not happen then or on any other occasion, except in the raven incident. That does not mean that it doesn't happen; it just means that it never happened to me. I remain open-minded on this issue. I do think it is quite possible. That thirty minutes was the longest episode of any of my Bigfoot sightings.

Ready, Set, Go!

On another Friday, I was about to change the tapes in the recorders, when I spotted a Bigfoot on the lawn. Since we were gone during the week, I think the noise we made when we got home on Friday aroused Bigfoot's curiosity. He was squatting down and leaning forward with his fingers on the ground and his butt in the air, as if getting ready for an Olympic running match.

When I opened the window, I may have caught him in the process of getting ready to run, either to the house to bang on it, or to run past the house without our knowing he was there. He turned his head to look at me. We stared at each other for about five seconds before he departed into the woodsy slope in front of our house. This Bigfoot was long and lean. From the top of his head to the top of his legs was around five feet. Add another five feet for his long legs. That meant he was at least ten-feet tall. This Bigfoot did not have a basketball-shaped head. He had a neck and a head that looked more humanoid.

Behind the Log

Another Bigfoot sighting occurred when Brutus and I were going on a walk up the driveway one beautiful Sunday afternoon. When we reached the pump house, the dog ran over to a pond area and started barking and growling. I slowly walked over to see what was going on. There was a Bigfoot, sort of playing with Brutus. The Bigfoot was peeking over the top of a log that had fallen at an angle. I could see the basketball-shaped head, yellow eyes, and black fur. When I appeared on the scene, the Bigfoot ducked behind the log. However, his legs should have been visible because the log was lying at a forty-five degree angle. He could hide his head behind the log, but not the rest of his body. I think this was another instance of Bigfoot making himself invisible, although I did not realize it at the time.

Another Log Sighting

One day we were coming home and passing the ravine next to the driveway. I always ask my husband to drive slowly, so I can study the ravine. Well, there was a Bigfoot, just lying on the ground like a log. I didn't remember any log being there before, so I kept looking at it. Then the Bigfoot moved his head and looked up the ravine at me. He just lay there and did not try to get up and run away or chase me. We just drove past him.

The Tea Party

Another time, while looking into the ravine from the car, I saw five Bigfoot. They were sitting down and each of them was leaning on a big fir tree. I could hardly believe my eyes. Five Bigfoot!! The way the trees were so close together, it seemed like the Bigfoot were sitting in a sort of semi-circle. I'm sure they knew I was there because they have such keen senses, but they did not look at me. They seemed to be busy talking. I wondered if they were telling stories to each other.

I had been grocery shopping. After I put the groceries away, I drove back up the driveway to see if the Bigfoot were still there. I wanted confirmation of what I had just seen. I also wanted to make sure they were not just part of the landscape. The Bigfoot were gone, and the trees they were leaning on clearly looked different from when the Bigfoot were there. The tree trunks were now light colored, not black, as they were when the Bigfoot were sitting in front of them.

The Meeting

Another time I saw five Bigfoot standing around the goat shed. This was directly across the driveway from the pump house on the west side. The abandoned shed had a tin roof, and a fence encircled the four trees that stood around it. The previous owners had kept goats on the property.

The Bigfoot seemed to be just standing around the goat shed having a conversation. They did not look at me, but I am sure they were aware of me. I think after twenty years, they were familiar with me and my vehicles. Since we were never a threat to them, they were not concerned with our coming and going. I did stop and look briefly, but a crowd of five Bigfoot is scary, and they were less than 100 feet from me. I went on home and stayed inside.

The Flower Pot

In front of our house was a compost pile that descended down the front slope. We put all our organic materials into this pile, which was not visible from afar. One day I was replacing old plants in hanging pots with new ones. I would take the old plants out of their plastic pots and toss them into the compost pile, saving the pots to recycle. I tossed the old plants as far down the slope as possible, so that everything would not be at the top of the pile. I tossed a plant down the slope, and right there was a juvenile Bigfoot I had not seen at first. I saw the poor thing lift up his arms to his head, because I had hit him or her on the head with the old plant! It must have been taking a nap in our leaf pile and leaning up against the soft, leafy pile of compost for its bedding. It just rubbed its head and ran off. That was the only time I ever saw a juvenile in that space. It was Drummer's space, and I could only assume that this juvenile belonged to Drummer.

The Five Stumps

One day I was driving up the long driveway on my way to a doctor's appointment in town. I was in a hurry as always, because I was running a little late. We had to allow a full hour to get into to town for any appointments. Once you drove up the driveway, you came to the locked gate. You had to get out of the car, unlock the gate, and get back into the car. After you had driven

The Locked Gate

through the gate, you had to get out of the car again and re-lock the gate, then get back into the car before you could start your trip into town on the two-lane highway. You'd better hope there was no construction or an accident that would prevent you from getting to your appointment on time.

As I was driving along the road from the house, I saw five stumps just past our fruit trees on the east side of our driveway. This was a semi-cleared area where there was only one stump. That day there were five stumps! I believe that as a camouflage, Bigfoot can make himself into an object that looks just like a stump. This was just like Big Red camouflaging himself as a split tree with the red interior showing. One of the species of Bigfoot on our property had a basketball-shaped head with no neck. I think this species might be able to pull his round head into a cavity where his neck should be, so that it looks as if he has no head. Then the Bigfoot squat down into a stump position. Their long arms are stretched out like roots extended from the stump. The tops of their heads are fuzzy. But all the stumps in the Northwest become fuzzy with moss on top of them. So this was very realistic looking. I stopped briefly right next to these stumps to take a better look. How I wished I had more time to investigate. However, I counted five "stumps." I am quite sure they were Bigfoot. Because I thought these were Bigfoot, I was able to assess some of the specifics very quickly.

When I returned from town, I made a point of checking the stump area. Four of the stumps were no longer there. Only the familiar single stump remained.

I wondered what else these Bigfoot had up their sleeve. I suppose they could have made themselves invisible, but as I understand from additional reading, this may take a lot of energy. Camouflage would be quicker.

Female Behind the Bigleaf Maple Tree

The bigleaf maple tree directly behind the back deck and directly in front of one of the tape recorders in the sleeping porch window is the space of a Bigfoot which I never named. This is the Bigfoot which must have been sitting in the backyard, enjoying the grassy area above the slope just a little outside of her space when Brutus chased her into the woods.

In one incident, Brutus came around the corner of the house barking furiously and with intent. He ran up the grassy slope and chased a Bigfoot through the woods. I was working in the area, so I stepped into the woods and onto an old timber road, and there was Brutus chasing a Bigfoot. Glancing to my left, I could see a juvenile Bigfoot about four feet tall. It was standing up on two legs and leaning slightly forward. The juvenile was watching what I believe to be his mother being chased through the woods. He was fifteen to twenty feet from me. He seemed very scared, so I just walked out of the woods and back to my project. My dog Brutus returned within minutes unharmed.

The Dinner Party

We had our hired hand, Barry, over one weekend to help with miscellaneous chores around the house.

He had once been a logger, so we had him trim all the trees along the backside of our house where they were growing too large and leaning in toward the house. We certainly did not want trees falling on our house. We had Barry trim all the trees along the tree line. The project took him the whole day.

As the day was ending, we were eating dinner at the kitchen table, when I saw a very large Bigfoot come around the corner of the garage, heading for the front entry door. I wondered if it was upset with our trimming the trees. One of the trees that was trimmed extensively was the bigleaf maple where the female and her juvenile hung out all the time.

My seat was at the end of the table, and I was looking directly out the window toward the garage. My husband and Barry were on opposite sides of the table looking at each other. As soon as the Bigfoot noticed I was looking at him, he ran back into the woods. I never said anything to either my husband or to Barry. By the time I could have said anything, they would have looked at me, and then they would have run outside and seen nothing. They would both have thought I was crazy. Besides, I did not really want to discuss Bigfoot with Barry or for him to know how prevalent Bigfoot was around the house.

Causing a Ruckus

We had hired a construction crew to come in and help us build a formal herb garden. The garden was to be a raised garden constructed of manor-stone blocks.

The crew was throwing gravel, moving large trucks, moving stones, using an electric stone saw, and yelling and talking. The herb garden was directly across from the bigleaf maple where another female Bigfoot, Stinky, hung out all the time. We were disrupting her nap big-time. I was standing in the herb garden area looking up the slope, when I saw this female Bigfoot walk past us on top of the slope across from the driveway. She walked past an open, cleared space of about ten feet, leaning forward slightly and moving slowly. Her arm was held at waist height with her hand palm-down. No one else saw her. However, that was proof enough for me that my hunch about this female was right. This Bigfoot was normally invisible to me as she hung out near her maple tree every day.

Up a Tree

This additional sighting was not on our property. We were driving to the beach along Ocean Beach Highway through Skamania, Washington. It's a pretty drive, rolling through hills and dales, passing a few scattered homes along the way and winding through a forest of Douglas fir. As we were driving along, I spotted a Bigfoot up in a Douglas fir. The tree was on the right side of one of the homes and growing right along their driveway. The limbs were about ten feet from the ground. A Bigfoot was stretched out in the tree, standing up. Maybe it was looking for pinecones in the tree. The seeds would be a nice treat.

As I have explained before, seeing a Bigfoot is an experience which you have to mentally process in slow motion before you can say, "Hey! I just saw a Bigfoot." What you do not say, or at least, what I cannot say is, "Oh look! There's a Bigfoot in that tree." So we drove by this event while I was still re-playing the mental video of what I had just seen.

I knew my husband was not going to be overjoyed when I announced, "I just saw a Bigfoot in a tree in front of a house we just passed. Could you please turn around?" Well, turning around on a two-lane highway with no shoulders is not an easy thing. I had to listen to his somewhat colorful vocabulary, but he finally relented. We turned around and looked for the house with the Bigfoot in the tree. It was gone by the time we got there, and I did not get a second look. This was, however, the first time I had ever seen a full-grown Bigfoot in a tree. At home I was always looking up in the trees for a Bigfoot, but I had never seen one. After this sighting, I bought a handy digital camera that I could carry in my purse, so I would always have one available.

This Bigfoot was black and covered with fur, including its face. It had yellow eyes, and the basketball-shaped head with no neck. We locked eyes for a second or two. It was nine or ten feet tall. It was not at the top of the tree, but at its lowest level, reaching upwards. The tree was about ten feet from the east side of the driveway and about thirty feet from the main highway. I had read on the BFRO website that someone in the Skamania area had seen a Bigfoot shaking a nut tree from the ground along the same highway. The driver had honked at Bigfoot, and the animal had stopped shaking the tree and walked away. I think humans really bother them a lot.

Amerind Foundation

The Amerind Foundation near Willcox, Arizona is a wonderful museum of southwest Native American cultures. The collection includes pottery and relics of their ancient lifestyle in Arizona. There is also a fascinating art gallery. My husband and I were playing snowbird one winter, when we made the journey to this foundation to see what it was all about. It had been a long drive from Tucson, so we decided to have a picnic before we started back to the city. There were some tables off to the side of the museum buildings in a pretty, secluded spot in the middle of some trees and huge boulders.

My husband was sitting across from me at the picnic table and I was looking straight ahead. Suddenly (of course, it is always suddenly), a Bigfoot started to walk around the large boulder in front of me and to my left, about forty feet from where we were seated. As soon as the Bigfoot saw me it ducked back behind the boulder. I could hardly believe my eyes!

There was a cave-like recess formed by the resting of one boulder against another and it appeared that the Bigfoot was headed there. Later, I walked over to where I had seen the Bigfoot, looking for other signs. There was a strong stench coming from behind a larger boulder on the opposite side of the sighting. I thought that if I went to the other side of this boulder, I would be face-to-face with a Bigfoot. I did not want this to happen. I looked for footprints but didn't find any, as the ground was rock hard. This Bigfoot was about five feet tall and cinnamon brown. It had fur covering its entire body, including its face. This encounter was very brief. Because of the smell that seemed to permeate the area, I think this Bigfoot was a regular here. It was probably its permanent space.

Backpacking in Wyoming

Back in the mid-1980s, our family went backpacking in the Wind River region of Wyoming. It took us three days to climb to the mountain area where we pitched our orange tents in the middle of a clearing, next to a tree. We planned to stay put for a couple of days. The group consisted of my husband, our son, his cousin, and me. The boys were ten years old. There were mountain lakes near this clearing and the three guys couldn't wait to go fishing in the closest one.

The lake where they were fishing was in a small hollow. I remained at the top of the hollow with a pistol in my hand. The three guys assigned me to be the lookout. The lookout for what, I did not know, and I do not think anyone else knew either. The wind was so strong that day that it just blew your words away, so no one could hear you. I kept watching the edge of the woods behind me because the birds were making a racket, a crowing kind of sound. I kept turning and looking around nervously because the birds would not stop making a ruckus.

All of a sudden, I heard a tremendous roar that made me tremble from head to foot. I yelled to my husband, but he didn't hear me because of the wind.

I was afraid to look over the edge of the hollow to see what had made the sound, because I was afraid it would see me, and if it did see me, it would consider attacking me. Whatever made that sound was not a happy camper. I feared being dinner for something in this mountain range.

My hand shook as I held the pistol, but I was ready if this animal appeared and threatened me. I thought it was a bear, and I was fearful of bears, especially hungry ones. Whatever the animal was, it walked past our tent, through the clearing to the opposite side and back into the woods with the birds crowing the whole time. From the sound, I must assume that they followed the animal into the woods.

When I told my husband about this incident, he said there were no bears in that area. However, he could see how frightened I was about whatever had happened. We packed up the tents and gear and walked back to the car by evening of that same day. On the way down the trail to the car, I saw a huge footprint in the mud next to a large boulder just along the trail. I thought for sure it was a bear and said to myself, "See? I was right about a bear." The print was ten or eleven inches long and four or five inches wide. There were no claw marks. I didn't stop long to analyze the print. I just wanted out of there! That would have been the best plaster cast of a footprint ever! Of course, I was not prepared for anything like that at the time.

When I look back on that experience, I am sure I know what made that tremendous roar and enormous footprint. Bigfoot! I knew nothing about Bigfoot at the time and would never have been able to figure out this scenario. I have talked to many hunters and back-packing enthusiasts and explained to them what happened; they really had no explanation of the situation either. I guess you just had to be there.

Chapter 7
Additional Incidents

Knock-Knock. You're It!

It is well-known that Bigfoot knocks on wood as a means of communication with other Bigfoot. Almost all of the knocking I heard in my woods adhered to a pattern—three knocks at a time. One Saturday night I decided to play knock-knock with Bigfoot. Our windowsills are wooden, so I knocked three times on the windowsill in our master bedroom. After getting no response for five minutes or so, I went about my business and thought nothing more about the three knocks I had made.

The dog was sleeping on a rug in front of the entry door, and I was in the kitchen nearby. It was about two hours after my knocking on the windowsill. Suddenly, there was a huge bang on the front door, and three knocks from the brass door knocker on the entry door. I'm sure this was Bigfoot playing knock-knock with me. I was frightened. I was certain that Bigfoot could knock my door right down if it wanted to. I never played knock-knock with Bigfoot again, ever. I was surprised that Brutus did not notice the animal sneaking up to the front door, especially since the dog was lying right there next to the entrance.

Up on the Rooftop, Ho Ho Ho

A juvenile Bigfoot decided to explore my rooftop early one morning. I was outside by the front entry door when I noticed Brutus looking up toward the roof and barking. I looked up to see what Brutus was barking at, and there was a juvenile Bigfoot lying on the garage roof. He looked at me with big yellow eyes and a very playful and impish expression. He had the round basketball-shaped head and cinnamon brown fur. He quickly scurried to the front of the garage, jumped down, and ran into the woods.

Later in the afternoon I was walking along the deck in the backyard. There was a mature alder tree up the five foot slope at the edge of the woods. The branches of this tree were bouncing from the top of the tree to the ground. I couldn't see anything because of the thick foliage, but my best guess is that the playful juvenile Bigfoot was in the tree. He was having fun playing in the branches, and I believe his activities were directed at me as a potential playmate. I continued working on my projects. I didn't go closer to investigate. Just as it's not a good idea to play with a bear cub because Mother Bear is usually near, so I was sure that Mother Bigfoot was very close by. I didn't want her to perceive me as a threat to her cub. Her reaction might be less than pleasant.

There was a roof-top incident when we first moved into our house. I could hear footsteps on the roof about three in the afternoon. There was a hallway skylight just outside our bedroom door. The blinds on this skylight were partially open. There was a Bigfoot on the roof, looking into the house from the skylight and making a whooping sound. Brutus started barking, and the Bigfoot moved to the edge of the roof and jumped off onto the slope behind the house. It jumped about 30 feet and ran into the woods. Although I could not see the jump, I could hear the thump when it landed on the hard clay ground. I looked for footprints later, but there was grass and the ground was very hard clay. The gutter was dented where the creature put its foot for the leap. I found a couple of similar dents in the new gutters on the west side of the house. From the office window I could see another dent in the gutter on the opposite side of the house. Maybe a Bigfoot had been sitting on the roof in that area and looking into the office window. Since the gutters were brand new, I can only conclude that the dented gutters could be the result of a Bigfoot's jumping down from the roof. There was another dent on the front garage gutter. This was at a lower elevation than the main roof. The dents had not been there before.

Walking on the roof was common behavior for Bigfoot. One night I was reading in bed. My two cats were curled up next to me, and my dog had made himself comfortable on the floor. We all heard footsteps on the roof. There were exactly four footsteps from something that walked up the slope of the roof. Both cats and the dog were looking up at the roof, alert to the sound of the heavy footfalls. The distance was about twenty-four feet to the peak of the roof. That meant that whatever had walked across the roof had a six-foot stride. Whatever was walking on the roof stayed up on the roof peak. I stayed awake late into the night listening for additional footsteps or activity of any kind, but there was not another sound.

Another time, as I was lying awake in the middle of the night, I heard something heavy walk across the lower front wooden deck right outside my bedroom window. The deck was also about twenty-four feet wide. Whatever was doing the walking crossed the deck in four strides. I wondered what would do that?

Roof walking happened often. I would go outside and look up at the roof and see nothing. I would go around to the other side of the house, look up at the roof, and see nothing. I put a ladder on the upper deck and looked across the roof in full daylight. I looked for a hair sample or any other evidence that visitors had been hanging out on the roof. I found nothing.

What I did find, however, was that something had dropped a lizard down the chimney. The chimney was a metal pipe for a wood-burning fireplace. The lizard jumped and jumped to get out. I could hear it repeatedly banging against the metal stove pipe from inside the bedroom. Of course, I figured Bigfoot had done this. Maybe it was the work of the playful juvenile. I didn't think a lizard would be on my roof, especially in the Pacific Northwest. The lizards we found in our area hid under rocks most of the time. Even a western fence lizard, if there were any in our area, would be extremely unlikely to climb that high.

The upper deck off the back of the master bedroom was furnished with a bench and some patio chairs. It was about midnight and I was home alone. I heard the chair on the back deck move. It was a heavy wrought-iron chair that would not be moved by the wind. I started loading bullets into our handgun. I was being extra careful, but my hands were shaking, as I was not used to handling guns. The possibility that I might have an intruder was frightening. Of course, Brutus was barking, so I knew something was up. I held my breath and listened for any additional noise, prepared to call 911, if necessary. Nothing ever happened. I think a Bigfoot was on the back porch and probably moved the chair by accident in an attempt to look into the back window. The only light in the house was in the bedroom. If there were a curious Bigfoot in the area, he left the deck, probably encouraged by the barking of my dog.

My son was on the roof walking around one day when we first moved into our home. He thought it was a cool thing to do, and, besides, there was a great view of the Columbia River. I felt uncomfortable about his being on the roof, so I asked him to come down. A half-hour after he came down, I heard something walking all over the roof again. I yelled at my son to get off the roof. He yelled back, "I'm downstairs, Mom.

I'm not on the roof!" So it was not my son this time. He was downstairs. Although I did not see a Bigfoot, what else could it have been?

Stick Signs

I owe a thank you to Lisa A. Shiel and her book, *Backyard Bigfoot, The True story of Stick Signs, UFO's and the Sasquatch.* Shiel explains that Bigfoot uses stick signs—sticks arranged in a meaningful pattern—as a nonverbal means of communication with each other and with humans.

I found stick signs left for me on my back deck and on the front patio. My husband woke me up one morning and told me to come outside because something had left an arrangement of sticks on the deck. He said it was definitely not caused by the wind. It could not have happened by itself! It was unusual for my husband to say that "something" did this and not claim to know what that something was!

I went outside to see what was up. There on the back deck were three parallel sticks about six inches long placed equidistant from one another, about an inch apart. An additional stick had been placed diagonally across the top of the parallel sticks. One more stick had been stuck in the corner of a rocking chair immediately next to the stick signs. At the time, I was so ignorant about Bigfoot behavior that I had no idea that the animal would do this. Shiel also suggested examining the kind of wood the stick signs were made from. She found stick signs on her property made from wood fifty miles away, a kind of wood not found in her area at all. Had I known this at the time, I would have examined the sticks more closely.

The next morning, the same arrangement of sticks appeared on the front patio. The only thing missing was the stick in the rocking chair, probably because there was no rocking chair on the front patio. The sticks were lying on the edge of the brick patio, which curves out from the front of the house and can be seen from the back of the woods. At the time I wondered about these stick arrangements, but had no explanation for them. I wish Lisa Shiel's book had been available at the time, so I could have been on the lookout for more such signs. Stick signs could have been all over the woods for all I know, but I was not keen enough to look for them. At least I was able to confirm that I did get some stick signs. The more we can document repeated behaviors as observed by different researchers and observers, the more we will know about Bigfoot.

In my collection is another book, which I cannot locate at the time of this writing. It told an interesting story about a man from British Columbia who was visiting a Bigfoot sighting area in Texas. He had been studying stick signs for years. He found that a Bigfoot had created a stick sign that represented either his name or just a designation for him as a particular type of human. He found his stick sign name repeatedly waiting for him in the British Columbia area. When he returned from a day in the woods at the Texas Bigfoot sighting area, he sat down in one of the chairs next to his tent. When he looked down at the ground, there was a stick sign next to his chair! To his amazement, it was the same stick sign representing him as he had seen in British Columbia!

Orbs and Unidentified Flying Objects (UFOs)

Much has been written about a possible correlation between Bigfoot and UFOs. I have looked and looked into our woods at all times of the night and day and have never seen a constant display of anything supporting this claim. When I say that, I mean nothing constant, nothing on a regular basis. However, there were two instances that were perplexing. There may have been more instances; I just was not there to notice them.

The first instance was something that sounded like a flying saucer hovering over our house. My husband and I had gone to bed at about eleven and were trying to go to sleep. Then out of nowhere, something came down over the mountaintop and hovered over the roof of our house.

Our house is situated at the bottom of a hollow beside a small mountain. The distance straight over the roof top is about thirty feet, helping me to estimate the length of the craft over the roof. The object hovering over the roof seemed to be about the full thirty feet in diameter and to be only ten feet above the roof. We could hear a constant whirring noise from the craft, as if it were moving around and around but holding a stationary position above the roof. I told my husband to hold my hand and not to move. The spacecraft hovered about five minutes over the roof and then flew over the edge of the cliff toward the Columbia River. As it flew over the edge of the cliff, there was a loud noise. Rocks from the two-hundred-foot cliff tumbled to the roadway below, as if some kind of sonic vibration had caused the rocks to fall.

A second time, at about three in the morning, I saw a bright light over the river. Based on the relative size of the tall Douglas fir in my view, the light was hovering outside of the cliff edge about forty to fifty feet in the air and about two hundred and fifty feet over the river. Whenever I get up during the night, I look out the window. That night, the very bright light that I saw suspended over the river and at the top of the cliff looked like a spacecraft. I felt that if it were a spacecraft and if it knew I was there, I would be approached. I tried repeating the words of *Row, Row, Row Your Boat* in my head, so that whatever it was could not telepathically pick up on the fact that I knew it was there.

To the best of my knowledge, nothing else occurred on these two occasions. However, they did happen. I don't know if there is a relationship between UFOs and Bigfoot, but if there is, it would not surprise me. Lots of strange things were happening, including my observation of an orb.

Orb in the Window

I woke in the middle of the night and saw an orb outside my open window. I had never seen an orb before, but there was no mistaking that this is what that was. It was orange-yellow and about seven inches in diameter. The windows next to the bed are jalousies. One turns a handle and the jalousies open and close. Both windows had screens on them. It seemed as if the orb were looking directly at me. I got feelings of anger and distrust from the orb, as if someone needed to check on me for some reason.

Suddenly, the orb jumped through the screen and onto the bedroom floor. I flipped on the light switch in the headboard immediately. I could see nothing. The orb was not visible with the light on. I turned the light off, and the orb was no longer visible. The next day I noticed a bright light in the left corner of my left eye. The light lingered in my eye for about two weeks. Then it was gone and has not returned since.

Now I know something like that can happen because of vision problems. However, the light was very bright, and I felt as if this orb had entered my body and was actually examining me.

I found it interesting that one week after this orb light left my eye, Big Red showed himself to me. The following week, Whiney showed himself to me. These two Bigfoot did not have to show themselves to me. They could hear the vehicle coming along the driveway, allowing them plenty of time to return to the woods for privacy. Did I pass the trust test, or what?

Maybe the orb was related to Bigfoot, or it was a Bigfoot spirit and it reported back to the clan about my intentions. At this time I was not recording any longer, as the tapes I was using had become unavailable. I was planning on moving, and I figured I had enough tapes anyway. My thoughts were not on Bigfoot or anything related to it at the time. I was focused on preparing for the move.

Chapter 8
Footprints

During the construction of our home, most of the area around it and along the driveway was cleared with a bulldozer. That left clear dirt for good footprint sightings.

I saw my first footprints months before we were able to move into the house. We were on our way to the Portland airport to fly back to Nevada. We had to walk up the steep driveway to our car, as the road was not completed as far as the house. It had been raining, and along the east side of the driveway, I saw human-like footprints in the mud. The footprints were small—about seven inches long. They each had five toes, plus an extra toe along the outside edge of both the left and the right foot. There were about four footprints very close together, only about twelve inches apart. Whatever had made these footprints stayed in the freshly-bulldozed dirt along the edge of the woods. There were no claw marks. My heart stopped because

I knew what they probably were. This was an, "oh-my-gosh" moment. I believe they were the footprints of a juvenile Bigfoot. From that time on, I continued to look for footprints. I found lots of them.

Over the next twenty years, I learned to recognize the different Bigfoot on our property by their footprints because each one's footprint was very distinctive. Some had an extra toe on the side of the foot, some had toes straight across, some had an extra-large big toe, some had a slanted toe line, some were very large and wide, and some were long and narrow. I think the last were made by a female Bigfoot. Like people's feet, they were all different. Although I could recognize the footprints after a while, I didn't know which of the footprints belonged to which of the Bigfoot that I had named from my recordings. I could recognize the same footprints in different places, however.

We rarely get much snow in southern Washington. When we do get snow, it doesn't last more than a day or two. One snowy day, Brutus and I walked up to the pump house, five or six hundred feet from the house. There was a pond next to the pump house. I walked past some berry bushes into the woods,. It was a beautiful day and very tranquil among the stands of fir trees and maples. I spotted a set of very large Bigfoot prints in the snow. They went from the woods to the pond. No footprints emerged from the other side of the pond; it was as if they had disappeared into the water. They looked fresh, and I froze. I wanted to show my husband the prints, but the dog was so excited to be in the woods with me that he kept running back and forth over the prints and they were ruined. They were about twelve-inches long and as wide. I was more than ready to leave this Bigfoot territory and get back to the driveway. I was too far from home and my safety net.

Looking back, I remembered seeing footprints in the snow while hiking in Lassen Park in northern California on a July Fourth weekend. We were staying at a cabin that we rented almost every year. There was a lot of snow that year. Along the roadside, the snow was close to fifteen feet high. We decided to go hiking anyway.

It was becoming difficult to see the trail because there was so much snow, and there were no trail markers. Then I noticed bare footprints in the snow. These prints were about ten inches long and four or five inches wide. I was sure the prints had been made by some vacationing college or high school students, since the park always filled up with students during school breaks and holidays. Walking barefoot would be a good way to get rid of some pent-up energy and to just be silly. Now I know that those footprints were most likely made by Bigfoot. At the time I had absolutely no idea what Bigfoot was. I had only heard the name. We ended up turning back to the cabin because it was increasingly obvious that we could easily get lost, as the snow got deeper and covered the trails.

The first few months in our new house I noticed a pathway being used daily, most likely by a Bigfoot or multiple Bigfoot. The path was down a slope next to the driveway, across the driveway, and down to a woodsy area along a two-hundred-foot cliff. Even though the ground was hardened red clay, Bigfoot prints were clearly visible in the dirt. The prints were not deep enough to cast in plaster, but they were distinct enough to recognize. These footprints were very large, about fifteen inches long and five inches wide. A round tomato cage in the ground next to this pathway had obviously been stepped on and flattened on one side. My husband said it would take extremely great strength and a lot of weight for that to happen. Well, it happened. I saw another footprint behind the pathway up the slope into the woods that matched the one on the bottom of the slope.

In the winter, elk enjoyed grazing on our lawns. Some of the elk weighed seven- to eight-hundred pounds. A full-grown elk can weigh up to one thousand pounds. Since it rained so much during the winter in the Pacific Northwest, the ground was usually very wet, so there were lots of elk prints on the lawn.

I went out to inspect a couple of these prints in the grass. I put my hand inside a print and my fingers fell into the indentations of five toes. Sometimes I could feel an extra toe on the outside of the foot. These were not elk gouges in our lawn. It was Bigfoot. It seemed that they were running, because most of the weight was on the front pad of the foot, with not much of a print from the heel. I did make a plaster cast of one. The cast was okay, but not special. Because I had been gone for six months, some of the footprints were old and had been rained on. Therefore, they were not the best for casting.

I did make another and better cast from a print at the side of the lawn next to the back deck. I poured plaster of Paris into the footprint, but I could not get it out when the plaster dried. It broke into pieces as I attempted to get the mold out of the hard clay ground. I made another plaster cast in the same area and couldn't get that one out either. The plaster cast was still in the ground and overgrown with grass when we sold the house.

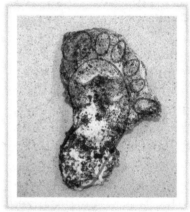

Footprint Cast

At last, I was able to get a cast from a print I discovered in the garden. I have kept this plaster cast as my reminder of living with Bigfoot. It is not a good cast, but at least I have one. The area was not good for casting, as the ground was hard red clay, and rain could ruin the footprints.

There seemed to be a pathway from the west side of the front of our house where the lawn descended into a ravine and faced the cliff in front of the Columbia River. Looking carefully, I could see indentations from Bigfoot prints in the lawn. This was one of the first areas where I noticed that Bigfoot might be traveling through. In the spring, tall daisies and grasses grew along the edge of the lawn, obscuring the ravine entrance. Upon closer examination, I could see that the tall grasses and growth had been pushed down, forming a pathway. There was an apple tree in that same corner with a block wall around it. I placed my tape recorder there many times and recorded what I believe to be Bigfoot. One of these recordings reveals Bigfoot pulling leaves off the bushes, eating them, and making an "ummm" noise, as if he were enjoying what he was eating. The bushes in that area had berries on them similar to blueberries. The next day, after one of my investigations, I noticed that many of the bushes had been stripped of leaves and berries.

There was another pond to the right of the entrance to our driveway from the main road. There was a grassy pathway around the pond, most likely made by wildlife. I thought Bigfoot might be using this area as a source of water. I looked very carefully at the indentations around the pond and found that if I laid my hand on the grassy prints, my fingers fell into indentations made by toes. The prints were large. This was in 1995. That was when I realized that Bigfoot were not only there, but there to stay, and they were roaming all over our property.

There were footprints in front of my hanging plants in the herb garden. It appeared that a Bigfoot had been standing in front of two enormous baskets of petunias that I had hanging from a tree and just looking at, or admiring, the flowers.

There were footprints around my beehives. I had three beehives up by the pump house, and I could see the footprints of a Bigfoot standing in front of the hives. There were no bees in the hives at the time because I had just moved the hives to Washington from Nevada. It was illegal to carry bees across state lines, so the hives were unoccupied. The different levels of boxes in a hive were kept together with hive nails. Something had twisted the hive boxes sideways to look inside and loosened the hive nails with force. Twisting the hive nails was not an easy thing to do. These same prints were standing in front of the gate which we lock across the driveway. The prints seemed to go nowhere; it looked like Bigfoot was just standing in front of the gate. The prints were mostly about ten inches by five inches wide.

Since our driveway was gravel, I would look every morning at the gravel to see what evidence I could see of possible events from the previous evening. One morning I could see the indentation of Bigfoot prints and a long drag mark across the gravel. I assumed that Bigfoot had seized a deer and dragged it across the driveway toward the woods.

In another incident, I had driven to the bottom of the cliff that our house sat on to watch the seals. It was salmon season, and that always attracted the seals to the Columbia River in front of our house. I parked the car on the cliff side of the road, as the fishermen were on the river side of the road. Our house was perched right over a great fishing hole. As I was waiting for the seals, I looked around for Bigfoot prints, of course. I

Cliff

wondered how they might get down the cliff and if they went to the river to fish too. There had been several reported sightings of Bigfoot swimming underwater and of Bigfoot fishing. I found a large print in the dirt. It was close to a cluster of trees at the bottom of the cliff. I wondered if Bigfoot had stationed himself there and came out to the river at night for water and food.

On the BFRO website, there were two sightings reported of Bigfoot in our area. One report said a Bigfoot had been spotted stepping over the guard rail on the river side of the road. When a car stopped to watch him with their bright lights on, the observer reported, Bigfoot just climbed up the cliff and disappeared. Another BFRO report concerned the property next to mine, where there was an old farm settlement from the turn of the 19th century. Evidently, there was an open water system frequented by Bigfoot. A child reportedly saw two Bigfoot drinking water from the pooled area. The author of the report signed it with his initials. They were the same initials as the brother of our neighbor from across the street. These two reports confirmed that I was right about this animal's presence on and around our property, and that I was not the only person to see them. After living with Bigfoot all around me for years, I stopped looking for more footprints, as they were always there somewhere and it was time consuming. But it was also fun and interesting.

Chapter 9
Sounds That Bigfoot Makes

This part of my firsthand account discusses sounds recorded on my property—sounds that I believe to be Bigfoot. I did send some .wav files of my recordings to Dr. Robert Benson, Director of the Center for Bioacoustics at Texas A&M University-Corpus Christi. In a program on the Discovery Channel, he said he could recognize the sound of any animal on this planet. He seemed like an appropriate person to contact. However, he said he did not recognize the sounds I sent him. He was getting ready to retire and was busy wrapping up some of his research. I offered to fly him to my property. He said if he were younger he might be interested, but not now. So I am flying on my own as far as my recordings are concerned.

These sounds are different from anything I am familiar with and probably what most people are familiar with. Many of these sounds cannot be heard with the human ear but the tape recorder picked them up. Because my recorders were running all day and night when I was outside working in the yard, I know I did not hear these sounds, but at the end of the evening when I played the recordings back, there were sounds I could not hear inside or outside the house. Of course, if they were growling, screaming, whomping, or clicking, I could recognize some sounds. As you start listening to the recorder, it teaches you to listen, and this makes you more aware; you notice more of the sounds in your environment.

I would put my recorder in a bird feeder with a roof on it and place it along the edge of the woods on the manor-stone wall that separated the jungle of the woods from our landscaping. I have recordings of Bigfoot sleeping, eating berries, thumping on his chest, drumming, clicking, knocking, growling, and more. In order to describe the bioacoustics of Bigfoot, I felt I had to name the sounds. Following is a list of sounds I have heard and/or recorded. Some of the best sounds were not recorded. Either the tape had run out in the recorder, or my supply of fresh tapes had run out. Here is a list of the sounds I have heard and/or recorded from what I believe to be Bigfoot.

- Howling
- Coyote howling
- Baby cry
- Chirping
- Pig snorting
- Bird imitations
- Whomping
- Whooping

I Have Never Seen Paris but I Have Seen Bigfoot

- Whining
- Hooting
- Clicking
- Low growl
- Whistling
- Frog sounds
- Imitations of planes
- Imitations of river boats
- Imitations of names
- Barking
- Knocking
- Chest pounding
- Rubber band high-pitched sounds
- Dinging sound
- Drumming
- Sleeping sounds
- House pounding
- Scratching inside the wall
- Farting
- Imitations of grouse
- Ooooooh ooooooh ooooooh (monkey-like) sounds

I'm sure there are more sounds that Bigfoot makes. I just did not hear them or record them. In itself, Bigfoot's ability to imitate sounds would probably make the list endless. Samurai chatter has been described by Ron Moorehead in his Bigfoot CD and book, *Voices in the Wilderness*. I was hoping to get samurai chatter on my recordings too, but I never did. I probably had a better chance of getting it when I saw the two Bigfoot walking through my property talking to each other, but I didn't get that on tape, of course. I think the more we can confirm each other's findings and research, the better we will be at documenting Bigfoot information. Because I was working in the Seattle area and not home during the week, I thought that Bigfoot would be more vocal because he had the place to himself. I will try to explain my experiences with what I believe to be Bigfoot vocalizations. I did not see him making these noises.

Farting

After I saw the footprints along my driveway, I looked for Bigfoot out the windows. The sleeping porch off the master bedroom looked into the back woods of our home. When we moved in, everyone in the family was outside in front of the driveway. A truckload of our belongings had arrived that afternoon, and they were busy putting the boxes in the garage. As I was staring out the window looking for any movement, I heard an extraordinarily loud fart. It was so loud that my black cat, Rhombus, walked over and padded up the five-foot slope to see what had made that noise. I was not hearing things. The noise came from right above the five-foot slope, only about fifteen feet away. It was so loud that it sounded like an elephant fart. I thought maybe it was an elk, but I would have seen an elk that close to me. Later I walked up the slope to see if there were footprints or any disturbance that might indicate what had made the sound. I found nothing. Later, however, I came to believe it was Bigfoot just watching us and invisible. I knew nothing about that at the time.

Chirping and Pig Snorting

Someone reported on the BFRO website that they had heard Bigfoot make pig-snorting and chirping noises. At that time I had never heard these noises, and of course, I questioned everything. Then one night, while I was lying in bed with the windows open, I heard a definite pig-snorting right in front of the house. The sound changed midstream into a chirping like a cricket. I have some of these noises on tape. Later, I was in my son's room on the first floor and could hear the pig-snorting just outside the wall. Again, the snorting changed midstream to chirping. I told my husband that it was Bigfoot making the sounds, but he ignored me and the noises and went back to his football game. I only heard these sounds a couple times in a twenty-year period.

Coyote Howling

One night I was watching a television program about Bigfoot. Someone had recorded Bigfoot and coyotes howling at the same time. They had some fancy recording instruments, which I did not. When I listened carefully, it was evident that Bigfoot started howling first. That apparently instigated the coyotes to howl in response. The program was timely. I went back and listened to my own recordings of coyotes howling and found that I could discriminate between the two animals, Bigfoot and the coyotes, on my tapes. Bigfoot howled first, and the coyotes followed.

Chapter 9 - Sounds That Bigfoot Makes

One calm and quiet night, I heard Bigfoot howl clearly over the valley in front of our house, followed by coyotes howling. Then, to my surprise, I heard every Bigfoot in the area howl right along with the first one. It sounded like a hundred Bigfoot lined up along our eight hundred feet of cliff frontage. I got the sounds on tape. I was absolutely amazed at the number of Bigfoot participating in this chorus. This howling started suddenly and ended suddenly, and I only heard it once.

Baby Cry

I had read reports on the BFRO of people hearing Bigfoot making a sound like a baby crying. Now this had happened to me, but at the time I had no idea it was Bigfoot making the sound. Autumn Williams, a respected Bigfoot researcher, made a Bigfoot DVD and got a recording of the baby cry at the very end. I don't think she knew it was Bigfoot at the time. On the DVD, she says something along the lines of, "There is no Bigfoot around here; let's move to another area."

I was home alone on a beautiful and balmy summer day. I walked out to my back deck to admire all the beautiful green things growing in the woods. I had just moved from Nevada, which is not known for its greenery. As I stood there, I heard a very loud baby cry. It sounded just like a human baby. I thought that maybe someone had abandoned a baby in my woods. The sound was coming from just up the slope behind some berry patches.

Since I had on shorts and thongs, I decided to change into jeans and boots to protect myself against the thick berry patches. As I went into the house to change my clothes, the phone rang. It was my mom. Since I am hard to get hold of, I talked with her for a short time. I did not want to tell her what I had just heard in the woods. Eventually I changed my clothes and went back outside. I was not worried about the baby, because the cry was a very healthy cry and not one of a baby in desperate need. I looked into the woods, waiting to hear the baby cry again, but I heard nothing. I stayed put and decided not to explore the possibilities. I thought maybe someone had been trespassing or hiking through our woods. My instincts said, "Stay here," so I didn't venture into the woods. I never heard the baby cry again. However, I am very thankful for the people who wrote about their experience with Bigfoot and the baby cry. I could not have made that connection myself.

Bird Imitations

I put my tape recorder in the bird feeder and placed it on the manor-stone wall of the vegetable garden in front of the house, right in front of where Drummer was always hanging out in his space. Early in the morning, I recorded what I believe to be a Bigfoot making the sound of a small bird tweeting softly, a sound which immediately changed to the sound of a medium-sized bird with a louder and longer song. And that changed seamlessly to the song of a large bird which was even louder and longer.

Chapter 9 - Sounds That Bigfoot Makes

My husband and I are both bird enthusiasts. Because I did not recognize this large-bird song, I called it the "Bigfoot Bird." I can always tell where Bigfoot is by this bird call. Sometimes Bigfoot is on the side of the house in the woods and sometimes in front of the house. This was usually where I heard the "Bigfoot Bird." It was a very inviting sound, perhaps the sound of a very happy Bigfoot. However, I only heard this bird song the first year in my new house. I never heard it again in the next nineteen years, which was disappointing. Maybe it was a visiting Bigfoot, and it had moved on to another space. I did get these sounds on tape.

Sleeping Sounds

One morning I put the tape recorder in the same place, right in front of the house where Drummer always hung out. This time I recorded what I believe to be a Bigfoot sleeping. On the recording, I could hear the rhythmical sounds of breathing, like someone sleeping. The sleeping sounds were of a large animal, not of a small one. The tape recorded this for an hour or more. I am quite sure it was of the Bigfoot who lived in the space right in front of the house.

Howling

The first thing I usually did when I came home from work on Friday night was to put a new tape in the recorder. The tape I left all week was a six-hour tape that was usually filled up by Friday. This particular Friday I was very tired and decided to change the tape in the morning instead. Of course, in the middle of the night, Bigfoot put on a howling performance to beat any of the others.

You can visit the BFRO site and click on this howling sound as recorded by others. However, it is not like having it right in your front yard directly in front of your bedroom. I think Bigfoot was not there when we got home, but arrived later and noticed our red truck in the driveway. When he noticed we were home, he howled long and hard, waking us both up. My husband said, "What is *that?*" I said, "It's Bigfoot." The sound was blood-curdling and made the hair on my arms stand on end. It was very scary. This was probably one of the best sounds I could have ever recorded, and I missed it. I never put off changing the tape again, but I never heard howling like that again. However, there could be some howling on my tapes, and I don't know it. I have so many hours of tape recordings that I have not listened to all of them.

I was standing on the patio by the back woods, under a bigleaf maple tree, when I heard sounds like large monkeys, complete with the *oooh oooh oooh* sounds, coming from the west of the property. This was the same area where I had heard the elephant-sized Bigfoot walking around. The sounds were about thirty yards from where I was standing. There was an old timber road that circled around the bottom of a mountainside, and I believe this was used frequently by Bigfoot. I was near Clicker's hang out, but did not hear from her. Once again, I did not have my recorder with me, so I was unable to record these awesome sounds. As far as I could tell, these sounds could be heard from the Columbia River below, as the sounds were loud and would travel down into the river valley. I could hardly believe my ears, as I had not heard these sounds before. Afterwards, I put a tape recorder on the back wall and left it out all night, but I got nothing. As a result, I started leaving a tape recorder in the office window, which faced the west side of the house, hoping to pick up some more interesting sounds. I found nothing on the tape.

Whomping

Whomping is a sound that I would describe as a sound that Bigfoot cannot help making. I have this sound on tape, as it is one of the most common sounds I have heard Bigfoot make. Early one evening I could hear a Bigfoot in the woods just behind a woodpile on the west side of the house. The woodpile was made up of trees that had been taken down to make space for our house. I heard Bigfoot trying to walk quietly around the other side of the woodpile—sort of stalking me. I knew he was there. He would break a twig every once in a while, although he was trying to move noiselessly. I was planting dahlias in the garden next to this woodpile. I think this Bigfoot was about five feet from me. He was on the downslope behind the edge of the woodpile, and I was on the upslope, planting flowers. I could hear the *whomp, whomp* noise. I think he would rather have been quiet, but the whomp noise was something that he just couldn't help making. I quickly planted a couple of flowers that needed to get into the ground and went back to the house, leaving Bigfoot with some peace and quiet.

Whistling

When we first moved to our new house, I would stay outside and enjoy the moonlight and stars over the Columbia River on beautiful evenings. One night I heard a loud whistling down the driveway toward the east woods. Having just moved from Nevada to Washington, I thought to myself, "Well, what kind of bird makes a whistling sound like that at night?" I thought there must be a species of bird I didn't know about in Washington. Then I discovered reports on the BFRO website that several people had heard Bigfoot whistling, and that it a was commonly known fact. I was grateful for these reports, as I do not think I would have made this connection myself. I heard occasional whistling over the years, but it was not common. The week before I was to move to Arizona, I heard a Bigfoot in front of the herb garden start to whistle, providing confirmation of the presence of a Bigfoot in that particular area. I whistled back, but received no response.

Frog Sounds

I would hear the sound of frogs in front of the house all winter long. The sounds would go on for hours. There was no source of water, no pond in front of the house. In addition, winter is not the time one hears frogs. When spring arrived, we could sometimes hear frogs around puddles or near ponds. But this ribbit sound was unusual for the winter months. We did have some tree frogs, but only saw a couple over the years, and they didn't sound like this.

Hooting

Bigfoot's hooting is similar to that of an owl. One day, my husband told me he heard owl sounds in the woods when he was walking around the property. I laughed and told him it was Bigfoot, not owls. Owls come out at night and don't hoot during the day. However, Bigfoot does communicate with other Bigfoot through this hooting sound. The sounds are lower to the ground and can be heard from one tree to another tree. I have this hooting sound on tape. Bigfoot will also hoot at night. One night when we came home from work, I could hear different individuals hooting to each other, most likely announcing that we were home.

Barking

Big Red, who lived up near the pump house, would come out about five o'clock. I could hear him barking in the woods when I was lying in the hammock closest to his area. He would bark and bark, not like a dog, but different. I don't know what else to call it except barking. I do have this on tape to help explain the sound. Big Red would bark and slam a heavy stick against the trees in his area. I think this was to let other Bigfoot know that this was his territory, so they should stay away.

Ding Ding

My tape recorders were voice-activated by rain, and it rained a lot in Washington. I was listening to a recording of the rain and thinking that I should make a CD of just the rain, because I always found listening to it very relaxing. Suddenly, I started to hear a very high-pitched dinging sound on the tape. Then I heard another dinging sound from what I assume was another Bigfoot. This went on and on. I have recorded this several times and have it on tape for others to hear. This noise cannot be heard with the human ear, but is an interesting sound picked up by the recorder.

Rubber Band Sounds

A very high, tense sound is heard on the recorder. It felt as if Bigfoot were observing me and tension was building up. It sounded as if something were being wound up and then released suddenly. I have many of these recordings. I once heard this with my own ears, directly outside my bedroom window. It was as if Bigfoot were looking in the window and my presence was making him angry, so he responded with this rubber-band noise. Most of the time, I heard this sound only on the recorder.

Scratching

I had read from another author that Bigfoot could transform himself and get in between the walls, where he could cause a scratching sound. This was another unbelievable story. I am grateful to the person who stuck his neck out and shared the true story about this happening to him. It happened to me also. Directly behind our bed in the master bedroom was a tall wall. The outside of this wall was twenty feet to the first floor, as there was nothing behind it. The front of the wall was fifteen feet from floor to ceiling. I heard scratching in between these walls, and I thought we had a mouse problem. After all, we did live in the country, and mice are a part of this experience. We were not home a lot, so I told my husband we had something new to deal with. However, I heard it only once and never heard it again. Obviously, we did not have a mouse problem. A problem like that does not just go away.

Chest Pounding

I have many recordings of what sounds like Bigfoot pounding on his chest. Often this was followed by his running up to the house and pounding on it, then running back into the woods and beating on his chest again. I would often go outside to work in a garden or walk the long driveway with the dog. Bigfoot was very aware of where I was and what I was doing at all times. He did not like me to be outside, since this was his property, so he would run up and pound on the house, then run to the woods and pound on his chest. It was Drummer who did this a lot, and the tape recorder was always in the front of his space. It was scary for me. If I were working in the herb garden alongside the driveway, I would park my truck in front of the garden with the door open so I could get into it quickly if I needed to.

I Have Never Seen Paris but I Have Seen Bigfoot

Once I heard the sound of a bullet hitting the metal chimney on the roof. A loud bang would accompany this sound. It would usually happen when I was outside. I felt that Bigfoot was angry, and this was how he showed it. My husband went up on the roof and found no damage to the metal chimney. (I did get the sound on tape.) This was followed by Bigfoot running to the woods and beating his chest, which I also got on tape. One day, however, I was in the attic moving boxes around and getting rid of stuff when I heard this loud bullet-sound on the side of the house, followed by the loud bang. This was not a gunshot. It only sounded like one. This actually shook our large house a little, but it did not hit the house. The sound was right next to me. I was full of questions about this activity. What was it, and what had caused it?

Low Growl

There is nothing like the low growl of a Bigfoot to shake your nerves. The first time I heard this growl was when I had just moved into our home and was walking up the driveway to admire all the trees and learn more about our new environment. I had walked almost to the top of our driveway, which has a steep side to it. A deer was walking in the driveway. I sat down on the driveway to admire the wildlife. The deer was not afraid of me, nor I of him. As I went a little further up the driveway, I heard a low growl to my right. It was the sound of something very large and very unhappy with me. I ran down the driveway, picking up a stone, in case I had to become David to a Goliath. I ran the rest of the way home.

Chapter 9 - Sounds That Bigfoot Makes

The second time I heard this low growl was when my husband had finished making the patio in front of the house next to the vegetable garden. I was outside along the edge of the lower slope to the front woods, when I heard the low growl. Into the house I went.

The third time, I was going up the stairs behind the house. The stairs led to the woods. I had my camera, intending to take pictures of the elk. They would let me get within twenty feet of them. As I started to walk into the woods, I heard the low growl coming from my left. One does not argue with this growl. I went inside. What attracted me to the back woods was that I could hear something going on. I figured it was rutting season for the elk and that was the reason for the sounds of anguish. However, the following day I found an elk skull that had not been there the day before. I think what I heard was a Bigfoot taking an elk down for dinner. I had just read that Bigfoot was

Stairs into the woods

Another time, I was in the garage sorting nuts and bolts left from the construction of our home into small drawers. It was early evening and a beautiful one at that. I was home alone and wanted to finish my project. The woods were very quiet. There was not a sound to be heard; nothing was moving. Then I heard that low growl. At the time, I had no idea that it could be a Bigfoot. I did not see a Bigfoot, but I remember the growl. Others have submitted reports to the BFRO that have also documented the low growl of Bigfoot. When I read these reports, I knew that had also been my experience.

A fifth growling experience came when I was lying in bed with the window of the back porch open. Brutus was outside, and he went into the backyard. I could hear the low growl of Bigfoot toward my dog. The dog, however, just ran up the back hill and chased whatever was there.

Imitating Names

I was walking toward the garage. The door was open, and I was going to walk through the garage into the house. Just as I was about to enter the garage, I heard the name "Otto!" And then again, "Otto." Otto is my husband's name. He was in the kitchen. I was sure that Bigfoot had heard me call my husband's name many times and had imitated the name. The sound was coming just ten feet from where I was, but I could see nothing.

I have read on the BFRO site that this mimicking of names has happened to people who live in the woods where Bigfoot is in residence all the time. However, this was the first time it had ever happened to me. It was an unnerving stunt, but probably also a complimentary one at the same time.

Imitating Planes and River Boats

My tape recorder was voice-activated, and sounds, including rain and wind, would turn it on. Small aircraft often flew past our house. I was told that ship pilots were flown back and forth from the Columbia River to maneuver ships down the river safely.

When a plane flew over the river, I could hear Bigfoot imitate the plane on the recorder before the plane even came near. It seemed that he could hear the plane before the recorder picked it up. He would imitate the sound of the plane, and then the plane would fly over later. This happened also with ships. The Columbia River is the gateway to the Pacific Rim. If you listen carefully to the tape, you hear first the imitation and then the sound of the real plane or ship.

Whining and Drumming

I explained whining and drumming when I wrote about Drummer drumming and Whiney whining along the driveway. I have both of these sounds on my recordings. I believe Drummer was using the skull of an elk or deer as his drum and a piece of wood as a drum stick.

Wood Knocking

It is well-known that Bigfoot knocks on wood as a means of communication. I did not know this in the beginning. I was sitting in a chair on the back patio under the bigleaf maple tree on the west side of our house. I heard a knocking, and I wondered what kind of woodpecker it was. Since I had seen woodpeckers around, that was a reasonable question. But after a while it seemed strange that a woodpecker would consistently make three knocks, then three knocks again, then three knocks again. Then I began to feel the hair on the back of my neck and arms stand up. I didn't know what was happening, but I left the area. Later I read on the BFRO site that Bigfoot makes knocks on wood. I had already found the footprints, so it did not surprise me that this could have been a Bigfoot. After that, I assumed it was. I learned to discern the difference between a woodpecker and a Bigfoot knocking.

It seemed that every time I went outdoors, the wood-knocking would start, going back and forth from one Bigfoot to another and then to another. Whenever I walked around to the west side of the house, which is surrounded by woods, I would always hear the knocking. If I were planting flowers, knocking would start. One day I quietly walked to the back of the house, trying to go unnoticed. I wanted to plant some flowers that would climb up over our arched trellis. I did not go unnoticed, however, and the knocking started. It is scary when every move you make in your yard is being watched. It didn't matter what time of day it was. In any case, I continued to plant the flowers even though I knew Bigfoot was watching me, and I could hear the knocking.

By the time we moved, there was a regular knocking on wood, and it was always in groups of three. One summer day I thought that a visiting Bigfoot was in the area. The stench was so strong, it made me gag. To me, it seemed that it must be a larger and older Bigfoot, based on the magnitude of the stench. The Bigfoot regulars had an offensive odor, but this odor was worse. I was standing on the patio in front of our house looking into the woods. This large Bigfoot was taking a log and smashing it three times onto another log. He was just below the log pile along the edge of the woods. For all I know he could have rushed at me, as he sounded very angry. I went into the house. I did not push my luck with this animal. I was only troubled once with this particular animal; I think it moved on, as it was not one of the regulars.

One summer there was construction going on at a building across the river. The workers were pounding every day, and they would pound something three times, probably to drive something into the ground. At least, that was what it sounded like. Every time they would pound three times, Whiney would reciprocate by pounding on wood three times. This would go on all day long. I could sit in the hammock in the herb garden and hear Whiney in his space, responding every time there was a sequence of three pounding sounds from across the river.

I Have Never Seen Paris but I Have Seen Bigfoot

I believe the wood-knocking sound is a vocal sound, not wood-on-wood. After listening to audio tapes of knocking, I think one of the tapes from Clicker's territory revealed the strong possibility these knocks are vocal. Clicker was caught on tape clicking nervously as I came near, as she always does. These light clicks changed immediately to the knocking sound and indicated they were clearly vocal.

This actually makes sense as many wood-on-wood knocks can be more of a thunk sound instead of a clear knock sound. It is my opinion that Bigfoot uses these three consecutive knock sounds to communicate with other Bigfoot. Sometimes this sound is needed quickly and in emergencies. But where is my stick? The vocal is quick, immediately available, and Bigfoot is very good with vocal sounds of all kinds. One of these tapes is available for you to listen to as part of this book.

Response to Ladder Against Pump House

The pump house was in Big Red's territory. It was a two-story building with a high-head water tank system. We hired a man named Barry to help with maintenance around the house. He was going to clean the leaves off the roof of the pump house and paint it for us. He slammed the long aluminum ladder up against the front of the pump house. It made a very loud bang.

As I was watching Barry, I could hear a Bigfoot scrambling through the brush. Brutus was barking furiously. I would have had to walk around the corner to see what it was that the dog was barking at, but I already knew what it was. I think Big Red was standing in the driveway looking at what was going on. He probably interpreted the slam against the pump house as an intruder, and he was on guard. I did not want to encounter this animal, so I waited until the dog stopped barking and Bigfoot retreated.

Barry continued to work at the pump house all day without incident. I never told him about Bigfoot, but I know he had his suspicions, especially about Drummer, the one that hung out in front of the house. Barry would spend the night with us and start work early in the morning. He would be outside by 5:30 AM just to enjoy the scenery before he started work. He told me that something lived in front of the house, because he could hear it moving around and it was there every day. I said it must be an elk or something and that I had seen elk in front of the house on this slope. I knew it was Drummer, but I didn't want to start that discussion. I also did not want it known that Bigfoot was hanging out near my house, as I did not want people scouting around on our property. I especially did not want people trespassing around with any firearms. I wanted to maintain my privacy and the privacy of the Bigfoot, out of respect for them.

Surveillance Cameras

I always wanted to put a window on the second level of the pump house and stay up until dawn with a night-vision camera to see if I could get a video of Bigfoot. It was a perfect setting, right next to the pond and about six-hundred feet from the house, in the middle of nowhere. We had electricity at the pump house that I could use for my recording equipment.

I never got my window, but I did put surveillance cameras on the pump house. They would record everything to a video recorder inside the pump house. The camera had a thirty-second delay, a very long time for filming wildlife. I would drive by in the car and wave to the camera, but my wave never got picked up on the camera. We got videos of my dog and of deer at the pond, but not Bigfoot. Technology was just beginning to blossom. Unfortunately, I was not a skilled technician. I invited two different people to my property to get an estimate of what it would cost to have someone install a system that would convey the photos to my computer. I thought that since I was gone so much of the time, the cameras would prove to be very helpful and provide interesting and easily-accessible video. Well, the estimates were about eight thousand dollars, and they would be laying hundreds of feet of electrical cable on top of the ground. I decided not do it.

I finally purchased a BuckEye Cam. It would take pictures in one-tenth of a second and send the pictures to my computer. The first day, I got a fuzzy picture of what I believe to be Bigfoot. It showed his arm and most of his body, but not clearly. He pushed down three bumper-pier ends used in my landscaping and passed right in front of the camera. I had trouble with the camera and had to send it back for repair. When it was returned to me, the company forgot to include the battery, which had to be charged. More time was needed for this to come together.

In the meantime, we left for Arizona for the winter. I wanted to leave the camera out the whole time we were gone. However, the battery needed charging frequently. I think it was only good for five minutes of video. I could have purchased a solar recharging cell, but there wasn't time, and it did not happen. I was hoping that my experiment would be successful, and I could purchase several more cameras to position around the woods. Just before I put up the BuckEye Cam, I said to Bigfoot—or to the wind, "I know you are there, Bigfoot, and I am going to get a picture of you!" It was almost as if he heard me and understood what I was saying. That is why everything was pushed over, and he was traveling at full speed.

Chapter 10
What Does Bigfoot Eat?

I have never observed Bigfoot in the act of eating. I have read reports from others on the BFRO website—reports from those who have seen Bigfoot killing deer, wild pigs, rabbits, rodents, and squirrels, for example. Because my major in college was nutrition, I was especially interested in Bigfoot's diet. It seems from reading and from my own observation that Bigfoot is omnivorous and will eat anything and everything.

I had just read an article on the BFRO website about a man who had seen a Bigfoot in his front yard. It was swinging a cat against a tree. It bashed the cat's head against the tree, and the noise it made sounded like an axe hitting wood.

I was working in the rock garden along the east side of our house. I had just put up a new birdhouse on one of the trees in the backyard. A squirrel had started to take up residence in this bird house. I was watching the squirrel from where I was working. Suddenly there was a flurry, a scurry, and leaves being quickly shuffled around. This activity was followed by a noise that sounded like an axe hitting wood. I never saw the squirrel again. There was a Bigfoot stationed behind a bigleaf maple right at the edge of the woods near the birdhouse. I'm sure that the Bigfoot caught the squirrel and smacked its head against a tree. My cat was with me while I was gardening. I took her inside and never let her outside again! This Bigfoot was only five feet from my back deck. Based on my recordings, that Bigfoot was always there.

One of my tape recorders was in the back window directly in front of this maple tree where Bigfoot hung out. Every time I went to the window to check the recorder or replace the tape, I could hear Bigfoot's discontent with my presence on the tapes. Even though the window was open, I could not hear this sound of discontent with my own ear. I could only hear it on the tape recorder. I would say Bigfoot probably would eat squirrel. The only time I saw squirrels regularly was when the hazelnuts were ready for picking.

One squirrel took up residence in a woodpecker house that was forty feet up in a Douglas fir. One spring, I watched a pair of woodpeckers in a confrontation with the squirrel living in the woodpecker house. The squirrel won. I would love to have had a pair of woodpeckers in that house.

I watched some black squirrels harvesting hazelnuts one fall. I had never seen black squirrels around our property before. There was a pair of hazelnut trees on the east side of the driveway. As I was proceeding down the driveway one day, these black squirrels ran to the middle of the driveway and actually charged at me while I was in the car, yelling the whole time. I was fine with the squirrels harvesting the hazelnuts. I just had to be careful not to hit one of them with the car. After that bumper harvest of hazelnuts, I never saw the black squirrels again.

Elderberries grew along the driveway near the pump house. I noticed that the berries were stripped from their stalks at the top of the tree. It looked like a Bigfoot had put the branch in his mouth and pulled it out, eating all the berries as he pulled the branch through his teeth. I assume a Bigfoot did this, as the top of the tree was about twelve feet high. This would be an easy reach for a Bigfoot, if he put his arms over his head and pulled the branch down to his mouth. The Pacific Northwest is berry country. Berries grow profusely everywhere. I didn't notice any blackberries missing from the patches we picked from regularly. We would pick berries and freeze them and in December, we would make blackberry jam. It was a matter of making the time. Picking blackberries is time-consuming, and making jam is time-consuming. We wanted to get the full flavor of the northwest, and the jam was the best. There were plenty of berries to share with the wildlife, but the blackberries went untouched.

One day, when I was walking up the driveway to the pond, I noticed that a three-foot oval of bark had been removed from a mature alder tree. It looked as if a scalpel had precisely cut this large oval. It was obvious that it had been removed intentionally; I am guessing for food, and I am guessing Bigfoot.

Chapter 11
The Bent Over Trees

Our property had tunnels of trees everywhere. There were trees bent over all along the side of the driveway and throughout the property. I have learned from BFRO reports that these bent-over trees are a possible marking of Bigfoot territory.

Trees usually grow straight up toward the sun, so when you see tunnels of bent-over trees, it's a good sign of Bigfoot territory. In addition, large trees snapped in half can be a sign of Bigfoot. We had a Douglas fir about twelve inches in diameter snapped off, leaving a stump around four-feet high. It was obvious that this did not happen by accident. If you are well-read on the subject of Bigfoot, you will see that this is a confirmation of similar reports by other observers.

When we passed a ravine beside our driveway, I would see trees that had been suspended in an X formation supported by other trees in the area. It was as if Bigfoot were trying to put a roof over the ravine in order to mark it as his own. At first, I thought the trees had just fallen and landed in that formation. However, the more I read about Bigfoot, the more I unearthed reports of this same sort of tree-marking. Observers remarked that this was not unusual behavior. Sometimes I would stop the car as I passed along the driveway and just look for signs of Bigfoot. A couple times I saw a large black figure move in the brush, as if to get out of my line of vision. I knew it was a Bigfoot when I saw it move. It had been hiding behind the brush on the ground. This would happen during their napping time in the middle of the day. Even when they were sleeping, they seemed to know what was going on around them. If elk were on the menu, this area would have been a good place to hunt one, as the elk herds often rested here.

At the bottom of a thirty-to-forty-foot woodsy slope in front of our house, sitting on top of the rocky cliffs, was a three-sided fort with no roof on it. My son discovered it as he was scoping out our property when we first moved in. He thought that someone had tried to build a cabin there, but never finished the project. I have read that similar dwellings have been found and thought to be those of Bigfoot. I didn't know that at the time, as I knew nothing about the behavior of the animal.

One Friday when I came home from work, I found a log laid up against the front door. At the time, I had no idea why it was there or where it had come from. My suspicions were focused on some of the teenagers in the area. We had caught some teens sneaking around the property bird-hunting and snooping around at all hours of the night. Now I know it was most likely a Bigfoot that put the log there to keep me from going inside or outside. Perhaps it thought it would make me go away.

Chapter 12
The Smell of Bigfoot

Bigfoot is often associated with an offensive odor. In Florida, Bigfoot is often referred to as the skunk ape, because it smells like a skunk. I have found the Bigfoot in my area to have three different odors.

The first and most common odor smells like dog feces. I could smell this odor in pockets all around our property. It was especially noticeable in the spring and summer months. There were pockets of this scent everywhere. When we first moved into our new home, I thought we had inadvertently built our home on top of an old garbage dump. However, this was not reasonable, as there was no old road to the property. The contractor who built the house for us had said we might smell some odors around the property, but they would go away after a while.

One day, when we were visiting the property with the contractor, he mentioned that the people working on the house had seen some interesting wildlife while working during the day. I asked, "Did they see Bigfoot? He turned around so he was not facing me. Eventually he said, "I am not sure what they saw." Well, there was a program on television that year that showed a clip of a Bigfoot with the basketball-shaped head coming out of the woods and walking about ten feet. There was a lot of verbal communication going on among some construction workers and when Bigfoot noticed, he turned and went back into the woods. I said to my husband, "That's our property!! That's our Bigfoot!!" The property was still cleared from the construction, as there was no grass. I recognized the trees in our yard, and I could see the Columbia River in the background. The clip was as good as the well-known Patterson-Gimlin movie clip taken in 1967 in California. However, our Bigfoot looked different from the Patterson-Gimlin film, in that ours had the round basketball head. I think the contractor knew about this incident and about the smells of Bigfoot and didn't want us to be concerned about it. I think he thought that as soon as we moved in, Bigfoot would move out. Well, that didn't happen.

The second smell was that of a skunk. The skunk smell of Bigfoot is not limited to Florida. We noticed the skunk smells primarily in the summer, and I think they were from Bigfoot visitors from other places, not regulars on the property. The smell was so strong you could hardly breathe. This intensely strong odor I associated with larger animals. If an animal is twice as big, I assumed it would be twice as smelly. The presence was dramatic.

The third smell was that of a sewer. Again, I only smelled this odor in the summer at a time when I thought visitors were present from different areas. The sewer smells I also associated with a larger or older animal, as it was so strong one gagged and gasped for breath. It struck me as something from a long lifetime of accumulating odors and Bigfoot's never being able to clean himself. This was analogous to someone not taking a shower for a very long time.

The Bigfoot that smelled like a sewer was the one with quite a temper, pounding logs on logs, instead of knocking sticks on trees. It seemed to assume that all the property was under its ownership and rule. This Bigfoot did not want us in its area. It was frightening, not knowing what this animal would do and knowing how much physical power it had. I was afraid to go outside while it was in the area. After about a week, it was gone and never came back.

Chapter 13
Conclusion

Bigfoot are everywhere. According to the BFRO (Bigfoot Field Researchers Organization), Bigfoot sightings have been reported from forty-nine states. If you want to have a Bigfoot experience, all you have to do is live in the country on some acreage and you will find yourself a habituator with Bigfoot. If you have a keen sense of smell, sight, and hearing, and a love of nature, you will find Bigfoot. They are curious animals, as they like to watch you, imitate you, and look in your windows. They are also mischievous and playful, especially the juveniles. There are only a few reported incidents of a Bigfoot killing anyone—scarring them, yes, but killing them, no. If you use a recorder, you may get some of the same recordings I did.

You cannot, however, just sit around in your tent waiting for something to happen. If you really want to know and understand Bigfoot, you have to live among them. In twenty years, they never hurt us, nor did they ever hurt our dog or our two cats. However, I was always careful to respect Bigfoot's sharing of the property with us. It was not all my property. Bigfoot also respected our use of the property, so we lived the life we wanted to, although I can assure you we were always being watched. Bigfoot have very keen senses, and they know what is going on around them all the time. It was clear to me the first time a twelve-foot Bigfoot looked down into my eyes with his big round yellow ones. I could tell he was very intelligent, especially about living in the wild. He was not aggressive about the situation at all. He was the one that left the scene, and grateful I am.

Those of you already living as a habituator (co-habituating with Bigfoot), please do not feed Bigfoot. The worst thing that could happen is for them to start trusting humans. Maybe you are trustworthy yourself, but generally, humans are not trustworthy with wild animals. Most people want to get rid of wildlife or use the animals in inappropriate ways.

If a Bigfoot throws stones at you, move out of its way. That is how you respect its space. Listen to the Native Americans and the First Nation people who are familiar with Bigfoot. They have lived with Bigfoot successfully because they respect the creature's space and its life. They share the wilderness.

The Bigfoot found me. I was not looking for them. Although they were probably not looking for me either, I have learned from them. Please do not harm them in any way. Don't kill them. Respect them and all wildlife, and please, *please* leave them alone. They are not monsters. There is never just one in an area. They have families depending on them.

If you were given a choice between visiting Paris for a couple weeks or you would be able to see, hear, smell, record and understand Bigfoot, which one would *you* choose?

Afterword

This book offers three new thoughts that I am aware of about Bigfoot.

First, the tree-knocking sound is a vocal imitation of what the sound of wood on wood may sound like. Bigfoot does not carry a hard, wooden bat around with him in case he wants to knock on some wood. Most sticks picked up at random would break, be too small, be too rotten, or too green and would not produce the consistent sound the Bigfoot community is familiar with. Also, there is not always a good tree to knock on at hand. As I recall, when I walked to the west side of my house, there were three Big Foot knocking from different areas. These areas were full of waist-high ferns, spindly elderberry and dogwood trees, and berry bushes, so there was not necessarily a big tree to knock on in their neighborhood. Knocking is an instant reaction to something happening in their area. It makes sense that a vocal process is most likely how they make it. It was the audio of clicker "clicking" and moving directly into the three knocking sounds that revealed to me that this is a vocal sound. Vocal sounds and imitations are what Bigfoot is good at.

Second, the Bigfoot on my property stay in one spot as their permanent place, twenty-four hours a day, seven days a week, three hundred and sixty-five days a year. They may leave briefly, i.e., for a couple of days, but they always return to their same spot. This was evidenced by recordings. When Bigfoot was not present, I would get nothing on the tape recorder. However, when Bigfoot was present, the sounds continued, and each animal had their own unique personality and therefore sounds to accompany it. An example is Clicker. She always clicked her tongue when anyone got too close to her. No other Bigfoot would do that. Another example is Whiney, who always had a low whine at different decibels. No other Bigfoot did that. A final example is Drummer, who would drum and imitate planes and ships on the river. No other Bigfoot did that. Each animal was unique.

Third, invisibility occurs in Bigfoot often. Bigfoot may be invisible more often than their physical appearance is present. Even though they are invisible, their body is still present in height and weight. This was profoundly evidenced to me when I was able to walk in the footsteps of a Bigfoot that became invisible right before my eyes. I watched as he walked along my vegetable garden path. He was present, then slowly became invisible, as he proceeded to walk along the path. I could walk in his footsteps, left, right, left, right, to the edge of the driveway. This was long after he had become invisible. I never saw Bigfoot disappear in a flash of light as others have reported. That does not mean it does not happen that way, it just means that it never happened to me that way.

Many of my sightings and experiences with Bigfoot on my property confirm what many other authors have reported. Examples of some of these behaviors are whistling, the baby cry, stick signs, gifting, imitating my husband's name, and imitating environmental sounds such as planes, boats, and birds. Many of these have been recorded on tape. Each time we can confirm behaviors and habits of Bigfoot, we come closer to understanding this very, very interesting animal.

I wanted to share my story about Bigfoot because it is unique and revealing. What I really want is respect for this animal, his territory and habitat. Big Foot is often portrayed as a monster and he is not. People are the monsters.

Appendix

Five Years Later

I re-visited the property in Washington State in July 2016. There were no Bigfoot around anymore. There was no trail around the big pond off the main Road, and the ravine was completely filled in with trees, with no evidence of elk in the area. There were not any bent-over tunnels of trees as before. What was there had disintegrated. Unless you knew they were there before, you would never guess it now.

The new owners said they have not seen one elk in the last five years. They have built additional buildings on the property, taken down many additional trees, and put in additional roads. In front of the house where Drummer hung out, many of the trees have been removed, and the larger Douglas fir trees have been de-limbed up to thirty feet. This makes the view of the river much nicer, but has displaced the wildlife living in that area. The additional building was put in the spots that Clicker and the large Bigfoot used as their permanent spaces. Because their habitat was changed, they have moved on permanently. An additional possibility is that if the elk moved on, Bigfoot may follow where they go.

My Opinion of Bigfoot

By Otto Moosburner

Are you kidding me!! I might have been open to believing Bigfoot is real, but not in my front yard, back yard, and everywhere on our ten acres of property! This information was more incredible than I could handle. I denied this information because it was truly hard to believe.

What I cannot deny, is that I saw the footprints, lots of them. I heard the screams in front of our bedroom window in the middle of the night. I smelled the odors of something that smelled like a zoo all around the property. I listened to some of the tape recordings my wife was making every day. Still, I did not want to believe this was happening. Here we were, on property that was planned to be our last resting place on earth. We built our dream home, which was also our retirement home. We had our house plans developed for twenty years. All our dreams were coming true. I was thinking rest and relaxation. I was thinking now we were able to have gardens and orchards and vine-yards and really enjoy what we liked to do at home. I was thinking this was a gift to my wife, as she included all her dreams into the house plan and landscaping plan.

We did do all of those gardening things, as well as hike through our woods, identifying plants and numerous species of berries. We also hiked in the woods with our two cats that followed us everywhere. We walked up and down the long driveway almost daily when we were home, cats coming along all the time.

Obviously if Bigfoot were present all over this property they could have made hamburger out of all of us at any time. We never carried a weapon or a camera. We just walked around thinking all is well. There were herds of elk on the property often and we loved watching them. The elk and deer were the only major large animals we thought were living on our property.

Although I denied the reality of Bigfoot all the years we lived in Washington State, I find myself encourag-ing my wife to tell her story of Bigfoot. I found myself listening more carefully to the evidence and the unde-niable tapes of sounds not known to either of us as coming from a familiar animal. The footprints, the smells, the sounds are evidence to open one's mind to the reality of Bigfoot, something we need to learn much more about. I find myself humbling myself to the reality of Bigfoot and how they managed to cohabituate with us. They never threatened us and they never acted like monsters which they are so often portrayed as. The more information we learn, the more protection should become available for these interesting animals which are part of this planet and they are here to stay.

Otto Moosburner

About the Author

Nancy Moosburner holds BS and MS degrees in Food and Nutrition from the University of Nevada Reno. She was State Director of Child Nutrition Programs for the State Department of Education, Carson City, Nevada. After moving to Gardnerville, Nevada she worked as Supervisor for Child Nutrition Programs in the Douglas County School District, later holding the same position with the St. Helen's School District, Oregon and, for ten years, in Auburn School District Washington.

Sound Recordings

Readers of the print version of this book can download the sound recordings referenced in this book from:

http://www.bookservices.org/AudioFiles.php

CPSIA information can be obtained
at www.ICGtesting.com
Printed in the USA
BVHW050726080620
581031BV00002B/7

9 781945 172755